T0272632

HOW to TALK

with ANYONE

about ANYTHING

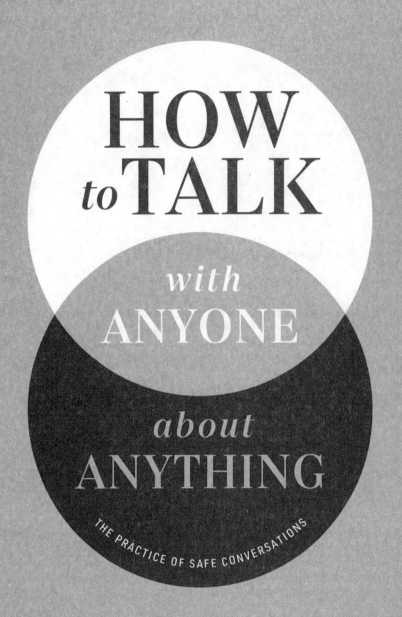

HOW
to TALK
with
ANYONE
about
ANYTHING

THE PRACTICE OF SAFE CONVERSATIONS

HARVILLE HENDRIX, Ph.D. & HELEN LaKELLY HUNT, Ph.D.

New York Times Bestselling Authors

W PUBLISHING GROUP

AN IMPRINT OF THOMAS NELSON

Published in Nashville, Tennessee, by W Publishing, an imprint of Thomas Nelson.

Author is represented by the literary agency of Dupree Miller & Associates.

Thomas Nelson titles may be purchased in bulk for educational, business, fundraising, or sales promotional use. For information, please email SpecialMarkets@ThomasNelson.com.

Any internet addresses, phone numbers, or company or product information printed in this book are offered as a resource and are not intended in any way to be or to imply an endorsement by Thomas Nelson, nor does Thomas Nelson vouch for the existence, content, or services of these sites, phone numbers, companies, or products beyond the life of this book.

ISBN 978-1-4003-3750-7 (audiobook)
ISBN 978-1-400-33749-1 (ePub)
ISBN 978-1-4003-4520-5 (ITPE)
ISBN 978-1-4003-3747-7 (HC)

Library of Congress Control Number: 2023945442

Printed in the United States of America
24 25 26 27 28 LBC 5 4 3 2 1

In 2010 in Abiquiu, New Mexico, we met with a group of our colleagues who were relationship scientists, therapists, and advocates. The group discussed ways to make relationship education available to the public so people would have access to learnable skills before they had relationships in crisis. This book is dedicated to this group, who named themselves Relationships First and adopted the vision of moving dialogue skills out of the clinic and into the culture. This vision evolved into an organization that became Quantum Connections, which trains people to teach our Safe Conversations Dialogue Skills in communities everywhere.

Contents

Contents

PART 3

PART 4

Foreword

We are honored to be invited by Helen and Harville to offer a foreword for their wonderful and practical guide to creating collaborative connections through a methodology they've developed over many years, Safe Conversations. We have both personally as a couple and professionally in our roles, including as a psychiatrist, attorney, educator, and mediator, found this method to be profoundly helpful in approaching challenging conflicts with a compassionate and effective way of moving from tension to more ease, disconnection to connection, and polarization to understanding.

In this comprehensive book you'll find fundamental principles, illuminating examples, practical tips, and relational wisdom cultivated by two heroes in the field of interpersonal well-being. Beyond their initial contributions to couples' resilience, *How to Talk with Anyone about Anything* takes us on a journey to explore how we can make relationships in families, schools, companies, communities, and governments more productive. If you're interested in learning to communicate in a way that goes beyond differences—while allowing people with differing opinions and views to stay connected—then this book is for you.

Foreword

In many ways, you as a reader may find these pages filled with moments of insight into your own creative applications of Safe Conversations that help you to expand on their fundamental building blocks of reaching out for time to connect, presenting an issue from a non-blaming "I experience" stance. Then the other, receiving person reflects back what was heard and offers statements about how this new understanding can bring empathic connection to the two in dialogue.

As Helen and Harville point out, disconnection results from speaking in monologues, not dialogues. A dialogue that mirrors, validates, and empathizes is the "royal road" to mutuality. Their emphasis is on how we speak *with* each other, as only then can we feel seen, heard, valued, and safe, both physically and emotionally. At a time when local, national, and global events are dividing families, friends, neighbors, classmates, and coworkers, we need the wisdom of relationship skills now more than ever to promote and restore connection.

Our human brains are built on millions of years of evolution, our mammalian heritage making us social from the very beginning. This two-hundred-million-year history of highlighting the life-affirming nature of our social connections means that we evolved to be in deep relationship with one another for optimal well-being. Yet when disconnection arises and we don't experience closeness or care, connection or belonging, our physical and mental health suffer. The quality of our relationships determines the quality of our lives.

On a global scale, what this means is that the polycrisis we find ourselves facing—polarization in opinion, disconnection as loneliness and despair, racism and social injustice, and even the destruction of our natural environment—may be seen as arising from the individualistic nature of modern culture. When our human identity is defined as only our skin-encased bodies, when we equate the "self" only as the solo-self of the "individual," then little focus is placed on the importance of relational connections. Instead, when we see the human mind as both fully embodied and fully relational, we can see that this is a case of mistaken identity that leaves us with a sense of hopelessness and isolation. As US Surgeon General Vivek Murthy has emphasized, we are in a crisis of isolation and loneliness with serious medical consequences, both physically and mentally.

Safe Conversations, so powerfully created and here relayed to us as fortunate recipients, gives us a way forward. By teaching us how to reach *out* to others and reach *in* to our own inner worlds, the structure of these invitations for connection by its fundamental nature is to create integration—the honoring of differences and the cultivation of compassionate linkages. Across a wide review of a vast array of sciences, clinical disciplines, Indigenous teachings, and contemplative practices, integration can be seen as the common ground of resilience and well-being. Whether Safe Conversations are practiced for the closeness of a romantic couple or the broader settings of companies and countries, learning to integrate our relationships with people and the planet is the pathway we need to bring a sense of wholeness back into our often-fractured lives.

Thank you, Helen and Harville, for creating and sharing this important contribution to our personal, professional, and planetary well-being. Those of us who read this book and apply its wisdom out in the world will be harnessing the "pervasive leadership" role in which each of us is capable—in whatever ways our skills and capacities allow—of bringing more integrative well-being into the world. Take in the wisdom of this shared mission and try out its practical suggestions. We're excited for how you will apply these practical and purposeful steps of connection in your own life journey. May we all find connection in the Safe Conversations ahead, and may we enjoy the journey to create a more collaborative and compassionate world.

Daniel J. Siegel, M.D.
Caroline S. Welch, J.D.

Introduction

Have you ever . . .

   . . . been upset, surprised, or shocked that a person you care about is on the opposing side of an important issue?

   . . . experienced judgment or chastisement for expressing your opinion?

   . . . been trolled or canceled online for speaking your truth?

   . . . left a conversation feeling victimized and/or exhausted?

   . . . wondered why a simple discussion escalated into an all-out war of words?

   . . . lost a job, friend, or intimate partner over a difference of opinion?

   . . . offended someone without meaning to?

   . . . felt like someone was talking *at* you, rather than *with* you?

   . . . found yourself avoiding certain family members, coworkers, friends, or neighbors because you can no longer have a friendly or productive conversation with them?

. . . felt like you were sticking your neck out every time you mentioned your political or religious views?

If so, you are not alone. As you have no doubt noticed, we are living and working in contentious times. Offering an opinion these days can seem like lighting a fuse.

If you hesitate to speak out for fear of triggering an argument or provoking criticism, you have a lot of company. Civil conversation has become increasingly rare, as has productive communication.

Look around a restaurant, party, or park, and often it seems that most people are more focused on their phones than on interacting with one another or the world around them. When we do talk to one another, whether face-to-face, on social media, or via texts and emails, it seems that conversations can take an ugly turn in a split second.

More than ever, verbal clashes seem to arise in family gatherings and during conversations at work, in social settings, and within organizations and groups.

Whatever happened to welcoming other viewpoints, or listening with empathy and understanding? Let's face it: most of us are great talkers but lousy listeners. Is this because we are afraid of what we might hear?

Pandemics, warfare, natural disasters, and political upheaval have driven us apart, isolated us, and sent us fleeing for shelter. Far too often these days, you may find yourself feeling stressed out, burned out, and checked out.

Clearly, we need a way to restore safety and civility to our daily interactions so we can talk to one another without triggering arguments or violence. Our method for doing this is to replace one-way monologue conversations with two-way dialogues that put you on a path to safer and more productive interactions and relationships.

That is why we have written this book: to offer you dialogue skills that will help you have Safe Conversations that connect you with others in ways that enhance mutual respect and understanding, and lead to productive solutions.

We developed these skills while spending decades as therapists and therapist trainers. Previously, our successful practice focused on helping client couples have more successful relationships by teaching them how to improve their conversations through dialogue. Now we want to expand that work by teaching Safe Conversations Dialogue to a wider audience with the goal of connecting individuals, groups, and organizations across society and around the world. Yes, we are so enthusiastic about our methods that we have targeted the whole of humanity.

The quality of your relationships determines the quality of your life. In these stressful times, many relationships have suffered because this information has not been widely distributed. We want to help change that.

Most people want mutually supportive, productive relationships in all areas of their lives, but many have not figured out how to build them. Until now.

Our Safe Conversations Dialogue process is time-tested and proven in therapy offices around the world with thousands of couples and in countless workshops with couples, individuals, and families. It has also been tested in educational institutions, religious organizations, corporations, unions, and international conflict situations with consistent positive results.

Our approach is so simple that there are only a few things you need to learn to transform your own conversations and interactions, even with those who may disagree with you. Our goal is not simply to help you connect to others so you can communicate calmly and without rancor; we want to improve the quality of all relationships across all divides.

Our History

We began developing the skills that led to creating Safe Conversations Dialogue in Helen's living room in 1977, when we first began dating. We had both gone through painful divorces, and we were eager to make our relationship work despite our differences.

One day, we were having an intense conversation that became heated. During the fight, Helen shouted, "Stop!" She then suggested, "Let's take turns. One of us talks, and the other listens."

Since this calmed us down, noticeably, it seemed like a good idea. So we settled down, taking turns speaking and listening to each other. This proved to be highly effective and much more pleasant than our own version of *The War of the Roses*.

The calm we felt was instructive. From the first time we tried this approach, we noticed that our emotions took a back seat to our intellects. This is a phenomenon called "regulating" in psychology. Self-regulating, or controlling your feelings in conversations, is generally deemed to be a good thing, even a sign of maturity.

In this instance, we coregulated each other, and the outcome was more profound and lasting than self-regulation. We paid more attention to each other's words and the emotions behind them. Rather than judging each other, we tried to learn from each other, embracing curiosity rather than anger or frustration.

It was a subtle shift, but the impact was profound. We discovered the magic of slowing down to take turns talking, listening, and seeking to understand each other at a deeper level. From our earliest days of dating, we shared a mutual curiosity about why our previous marriages had failed. We wanted to avoid making the same mistakes. We shared an emotional and intellectual interest about what it takes to create a healthy relationship since we both have degrees in psychology and therapy, and we understood a lot about human behavior.

In our discussions about our personal situations, we came to realize that while we were creative and accomplished people, we also were vulnerable and defensive. Even though we cared about each other, we had conflicts similar to those in our previous marriages—and our conflicts were similar to those we each had in our childhoods with our caretakers. That was a shocking discovery.

As therapists, we'd thought initially that the answer to helping two people connect was to teach them how to practice conflict resolution by problem-solving, which was the main methodology of the marital therapy profession at that time. Later, we realized that the baggage we carry from our pasts can interfere with how we connect in our adult relationships.

Then we made two important discoveries: First, the problem behind tension and conflict is that everyone seems to "object to difference." All too often, when we try to talk with others about things on which we differ, we struggle because of *how* we talk to each other, not *what* we talk about.

Second, the tension and conflict caused by our objection to differences produces polarization and disconnection. Since this seems to be the human condition, and not unique to us, it's probably true for you and most others.

Introduction

We have built our lives around sharing these discoveries through our Imago Relationship Therapy clinical practice, our couples' workshops, and in our training of other professionals.

Our work served as the foundation for our bestselling book *Getting the Love You Want*, which was first published in 1988. Oprah Winfrey became a big fan of the book and featured it seventeen times on her show. It became a *New York Times* bestseller eleven times and has sold more than four million copies to date. We've written ten more books and workbooks, including two more *New York Times* bestsellers.

Oprah told her millions of viewers that our book helped change her view of relationships from a romantic pursuit to a spiritual partnership that's meant to change how you see yourself and the world.[1]

We felt even more validated when recording artist Alanis Morissette joined Oprah to share the impact our book and therapy methods had on her life too. Both characterized *Getting the Love You Want* as the best relationship book in the world—ever.

With this book, we are expanding our outreach beyond couples to a larger audience by offering guidance on how to improve relationships in all areas of your life. In the pages that follow, you will learn a skill called Safe Conversations (SC) Dialogue that will help you talk with anyone about anything.

This skill will help you create safety so you can connect and have conversations without feeling like you are lighting a fuse. We will provide ways to feel safe even during serious disagreements.

You will learn how to discuss contentious topics without fear of conflict. We will teach you a simple set of practices that will help you connect with family, friends, coworkers, and everyone with whom you interact. The goal is to help you communicate with them without polarization or conflict.

Yes! That is possible.

You have a choice. You can avoid or shut out everyone who ruffles your feathers, disagrees with you, or threatens your perspective, or you can learn to accept differing views by tapping into your curiosity and embracing empathy.

We tell our clients that how you look at others determines what you see in them. It's obvious once you think about it! We invite you to join us in listening to others without judgment and instead curiosity. You can always decide later on whether you will accept what they say, but even if you don't, you can still be empathic toward them.

Nearly eighty years of research indicates that we physically and mentally thrive when we feel secure in our relationships.[2] Good relationships can make us live longer and more happily. Perhaps that is why connection is a deep human yearning. It is good for our survival. When we feel safe, we naturally care for other individuals and for the whole of humanity. We have a greater capacity to love.

The Problem with Wanting to Be the Best

The most common and traditional value system of our culture, especially in the United States, is to *be the best*, for all sorts of positive reasons. Growing up, young people are encouraged to be the best by getting top grades, excelling at sports, landing a star role in a school play, becoming first chair in the orchestra, or otherwise standing out. We are told that if we rank among the best, we will be accepted by a college so we can earn a degree, make a good living, and live happily ever after.

Yet in our drive to be the best, we tend to become assertive in expressing our thoughts and opinions. We learn to speak in monologues, expecting others to listen and agree with us. We think that is how confident and accomplished people communicate.

But speaking in that way is not the most effective way to converse if you hope to make connections and build lasting relationships.

When you speak in a monologue, you aren't conversing; you are speechifying. The monologuist is not looking to be understood as much as to be recognized as an authority and a leader.

When we speak in monologues, we tend to trigger disagreement and conflict rather than agreement and cooperation because we speak as though only our views have merit. We are not open to other ideas or opinions. This is why the person who speaks in monologues cannot talk to others without judging them, disagreeing, and becoming angry and frustrated.

We all want to be seen, heard, and valued. These are basic human needs, the oxygen and perfume of life. When these needs are not met, we do bad things to others or to ourselves—or both—to get those needs met, even if negatively. We fulfill these needs when we communicate through dialogues that feature an exchange of views rather than monologues that offer only the speaker's one-sided viewpoint. By communicating only through monologues, you may survive, but you cannot thrive—and neither can humanity.

The absence of dialogue results in the conflict and polarization we are experiencing in our culture and around the world today. This escalation of anger, interpersonal conflict, and polarization suppresses life energy and causes many to withdraw into depression, despair, hopelessness, and sometimes to commit suicide. Our Safe Conversations Dialogue process allows you to be seen, heard, and valued, thus fulfilling the needs we all share.

Neither of us could have predicted that Helen's intervention during one of our early arguments as a couple was the beginning of something that would be transformative for everyone. In fact, this more thoughtful approach became the seed that ultimately grew into Safe Conversations Dialogue, which we will call SC Dialogue from here on out. This set of skills became our primary way of working with couples and has transformed thousands of lives across the world, and we believe it will transform millions more, if not billions.

In this book and its accompanying workbook, we are taking SC Dialogue to the next level—from a skill set for improving the relationship of couples to one that will change our global culture. Our SC Dialogue skills will help you create productive conversations that restore connection rather than cause conflict. Our process has proven to be life-changing for our readers and clients. The value of using SC Dialogue is that it's relevant to all human ecosystems. The skills can be applied in corporations, educational systems, religious institutions, politics, and families.

SC Dialogue addresses the current phenomenon of personal and systemic polarization by offering a new way to talk without criticism, to listen without judgment, and to connect beyond our differences. We all need to live with, understand, and accept our differences with one another, since differences will always exist. They are the defining feature of nature. There is no "sameness" in the universe, only similarity. This book will give you skills and strategies that will help you feel safe and valued even when you disagree with someone.

We visualize a world where our differences—no matter our social, cultural, or political backgrounds—do not stand in the way of connection. They give birth to new ways to make it possible. In that safer world, you can embrace different views as a path to greater understanding and empathy.

Introduction

We invite you to experience the joy of making SC Dialogue part of your daily life; then you can share what you have learned with others. Practice it with your partner, friends, children, and family members. Take it to work, to your place of worship, to your classroom, and to your community. It can transform all your relationships in all your environments.

SC Dialogue makes it possible for anyone to talk with anyone about anything. It is a skill you can learn and practice. It is a new way to converse that makes it possible for all points of view to be expressed and heard without conflict or polarization. We have a choice: to polarize around difference, or to use the tension of difference to generate enormous creativity.

We see these skills as driving a global social movement that we hope will replace a culture focused on individual achievement with one that focuses on relationship and encourages collaboration, cooperation, and interdependency. When we can work and live together despite our differences, we will be on a path to a new relational civilization that values universal freedom, full equality for everyone, the celebration of difference, and total inclusiveness.

Our goal is to create a better world where we shift from conflict to connection, from winning to creating win-wins—a world where we put relationships first. We want to usher in a new global relational civilization, and we invite you to embrace SC Dialogue and share it with others.

Harville Hendrix, PhD
Helen LaKelly Hunt, PhD

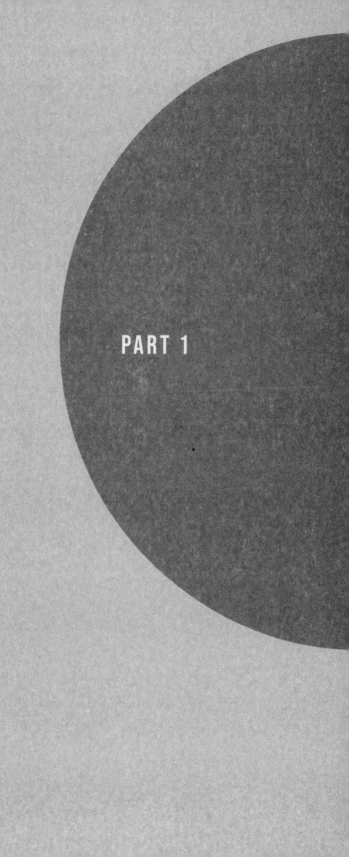

PART 1

CHAPTER 1

The Problem

In a 2023 interview with the *Guardian*, a Washington, DC, think-tank adviser summed up the current crisis of disconnection in public conversations and communication breakdowns across all societal ecosystems. He was asked about the controversy over the origins of the pandemic, but his response could be applied to almost any issue of the day.

"Isn't this just like everything else in American politics, where a partisan position on one side invites a partisan response by the other? There's a lot of what might be called reactive thinking going on because of the high degree of polarization and the high stakes. Charges without foundation invite responses without foundation. . . . If this isn't lifted out of the crucible of political debate right now, it'll just get worse and worse."[1]

The think-tank adviser made a good point.

Whatever happened to discussions that led to solutions? Or safe and civil conversations that reached an amicable conclusion? When was the last time you had an enlightening and fruitful talk with someone about a topic upon which you disagreed?

In our increasingly polarized society, talking often seems to be the most dangerous thing we can do. The problem isn't poor communication so much as it is the disconnection that results when we speak to one another in monologues rather than dialogues.

Not being seen, heard, and valued triggers the painful sensation of anxiety; our defenses are activated, and we become polarized. In dialogue, on the other hand, we speak "with" each other. When a person feels seen, heard, and valued, they feel safe physically and emotionally, which promotes connection. Connection makes it okay to be vulnerable and makes true communication possible.

We need to move away from monologue, where we talk *at* each other. Our Safe Conversations Dialogue model helps you communicate with others on an equal level that is mutually engaging and more productive. We believe it is the path to a better future for all of us.

When you consider the sharp political divisions and polarizations that have ruined friendships and left critical issues unresolved in recent years, the need for finding a better way to communicate is a no-brainer. In the past, some political leaders of opposing parties—for example, in 2015 President Barack Obama worked with Republicans and Democrats to pass the first transportation spending bill in a decade—put aside their ideological differences and worked out agreements for the benefit of the country. Increasingly, though, the common good is trampled by a winner-takes-all environment. This is the result of a disconnection between individuals and our social systems.

"Winning becomes the goal over almost every other consideration," a report by the Brookings Institution noted.[2] We see that value system as dysfunctional in our society.

The report also explained that in such a toxic environment,

there seems to be little room for productive discussion or debate. "Liberals see conservatives limiting voting rights, endangering democracy, and ignoring procedural safeguards, while conservatives think progressives are turning to socialism and disrespecting freedom and liberty. Viewing others with great suspicion and doubting their motives is an indication that faith in the system is eroding and there is little good will in how people deal with one another," the same report concluded.[3]

We are bombarded daily with news reports of increasing incidents of road rage, violence in the workplace, and heightened day-to-day tensions at public meetings, schools, and commercial spaces. And if you are a frequent flyer, these days you may feel like your passenger seat is ringside at a mixed martial arts match.

"Today when flight attendants put on their uniforms, they don't know if it's going to be a signal of leadership and authority for safety in the cabin or a target for a violent attack," Sara Nelson, head of the Association of Flight Attendants, recently told CNN.[4]

Before 2021, the FAA had seen little change in annual investigations of reports of unruly passenger incidents, but the CNN article notes that 2021 brought a nearly 500 percent increase over the historic average, prompting the federal agency to institute a zero-tolerance campaign. "We also have a lot of incidents that are happening more regularly that are violent maybe not directly toward someone, but in actions and words: punching backs of seats, spitting, throwing trash at people, yelling obscenities, using racial, gender and homophobic slurs," Nelson told CNN.[5]

Whether in online chat rooms disrupted by insults and foul language, dinner conversations that disintegrate into arguments, or congressional debates where elected officials shout down one other, public discourse too often unravels into threats and rants meant to defame, degrade, and diminish the other side.

If you need further proof of the breakdown in civil discourse, spend a few minutes scrolling social media and you will find ample evidence that ranting is far more prevalent than rational discussions. Competition for control as the social narrative has replaced collaboration, cocreation, and cooperation in working together toward shared goals.

Conversation was once considered a social art; now it is more like a martial art. When not distracted and in a resting state, we listen with only a 13 to 18 percent accuracy rate. It often seems listening is in danger of becoming a lost art.[6] Apparently, our ears did not evolve as well as our vocal cords.

Our ability to communicate in a way that connects us with one another elevates humans from other species; yet if talking to each other triggers animosity and violence, we may not be a superior species after all.

The Toll of Disconnection and Uncivil Discourse

Most of us have felt invisible, unheard, devalued, and disconnected at one time or another. The fact is that we are wired to connect. It is not something we can do or stop doing. We are connecting beings. It is our nature.

So why have so many of us experienced disconnection in recent times? We have become polarized politically and socially to the point that many feel they are invisible and vulnerable. In response, they go into self-protection mode and become defensive, because we all need to feel that we are valued and part of something bigger than ourselves.

Historically, our survival has depended on cooperation and

collective action. And it still does. Strong connections and open communication are vital for success and meaningful relationships, including at work, in school, in the community, and in our places of worship.

When a disconnection distorts communication, it often breaks down into confrontation, whether face-to-face, on the phone, or online via emails, texts, and chats. Then we become stressed and less likely to have healthy relationships, productive careers, overall good health, and a sense of well-being.

Have you ever suggested something to a friend or coworker and received a dismissive or rude response? How did that make you feel? Angry? Upset? Stressed out?

You certainly did not feel capable of being your best or doing your best, did you? Living or working in a combative setting can have a negative impact on your cognitive abilities and mental health.

Breakdowns in communication result in confrontations rather than conversations. When we don't listen to each other and instead interrupt, interject, or cut off conversation with threats and insults, we disconnect. And when we cannot work together to solve common problems, our relationships suffer, productivity declines, and, in far too many cases, the result is open conflict and even violence or chaos.

The Problem Behind the Problem

At her annual checkup, Sarah asked her doctor whether the blood pressure medicine she was taking might be giving her anxiety.

She told her doctor:

"I found an article on the Mayo Clinic website that said—"

But her doctor interrupted and shut Sarah down before she could complete her sentence.

"You don't know what you're talking about," the physician said curtly.

Welcome, Sarah, to a classic "psychic annihilation." Now, that may sound like the title of a new Marvel superhero movie, but it is a very real thing and an all-too-common experience, especially in these tempestuous times.

A psychic annihilation occurs when someone dismisses another person's point of view simply because it conflicts with their own. In this case, maybe the doctor felt that, after seven-plus years of medical education and twenty years as a general practitioner, he knew more about Sarah's blood pressure medicine than someone who spent five minutes googling it. But by cutting off Sarah so rudely and dismissively, the doctor damaged their relationship and possibly lost a patient in the process.

From our perspective, we see all of these conflicts and polarizations as symptoms, not the problem. These symptoms are indications that the basic human need to be seen, heard, and valued is not being met. They are the result of the failure of our social and economic systems.

So no matter how many symptoms we address and remove, they will continue to show up until the system transforms to care for and respond to the welfare of the whole.

Next, let's look at the *problem* behind the problems. To make sense of *why* we human beings cause each other so much pain and suffering, we need to understand the human condition, especially its tragic dimension. What do we mean by the *tragic dimension* of our existence?

We live in a connecting universe, and in that universe, all

human beings are connecting with all other human beings, all the time and everywhere, as well as with all of nature and the cosmos. This perspective is rooted in ancient traditions and in the newest and most accurate scientific discipline, or view of nature, that we humans have developed—quantum physics.

A thesis of the quantum sciences is that the universe is a field of energy that is self-aware and creative.[7] All things we know and see—like galaxies, solar systems, planets, particles, atoms, cells, and all life forms—arise out of, and exist in, that field.

We are self-aware and creative because we are made out of this invisible self-aware energy that constantly gives birth to forms that make up the visible world we experience. We call this the *wonder of being*. When we experience our connectedness to this source, we experience the wonder of being, and ourselves as wondrous beings.

We believe that wonder, experienced as joyful aliveness, is our true nature. But we have species amnesia. Most of us are not consciously aware of this. To stimulate that awareness, we declare this reality to our audience at the start of every public presentation. We want to remind them, and now you, about who we are, since most of us have forgotten. To do this, we point toward the crowd—face-to-face or on Zoom—and declare firmly: "You are wonderful, and that is the truth." Then we instruct our audience to point to the person next to them—to their spouse, colleague, child, friend, or the Zoom participants—and shout, "You are wonderful!" followed by pointing to themselves and saying, "I am wonderful" and then to all of us, "We are wonderful, and that's the truth!" Then we start our presentation and repeat this ritual at the end.

William Wordsworth, a great English poet, alluded to our being a part of the whole cosmos in this excerpt from his poem

"Ode: Intimations of Immortality from Recollections of Early Childhood":

> But trailing clouds of glory do we come
> . . . .
> Heaven lies about us in our infancy!
> Shades of the prison-house begin to close
> Upon the growing Boy,
> . . . .
> He sees it in his joy;
> . . . .
> And by the vision splendid
> Is on his way attended;
> At length the Man perceives it die away,
> And fade into the light of common day.[8]

What Wordsworth meant, and we agree, is that in our original condition, we human beings are glorious creatures who not only live in but are also a part of the cosmos. That is our true nature. We would add that our primary sensations when we are experiencing the cosmos are joyfulness and deep relaxation.

Children play with abandon naturally, but if something painful happens, they can become anxious, lose their spontaneity, and become defensive. This was demonstrated with chilling clarity in a research project at the University of Massachusetts Boston in which a child psychiatrist filmed interactions between a nine-month-old infant and her mother/caretaker in what the psychiatrist called the still-face experiment. In it, the mother and child experience a joyful connection while making sounds and looking at objects in the room. Then the researcher asks the mother to break eye contact and look away from her infant.

Then she looks back at the infant with a still face, offering no expression at all. Her infant notices this and tries to engage again by making a gurgling sound and pointing to objects in the room.

As the mother maintains her blank expression, her infant tries harder and harder to get her attention. Failing to do so, the infant becomes agitated, turns away, and then turns back. The child next goes into a panic and body contractions, crying in despair. After ten seconds of this, the researcher instructs the mother to reengage by echoing her child's earlier joyful sound by smiling, pointing, and making other comforting sounds.

The baby stops panicking, looks at the mother for a few seconds, and then, with some hesitancy, reengages in their play with giggles and joy. The ruptured connection is restored, but the baby now has a memory that such a wonderful experience could be lost. Anxiety has entered its world. Joyful aliveness, as a constant state, has been lost.

The connection between the mother and child was ruptured by the mother. In the research, she abruptly turns away and then turns back with a "still face." In real life, this sort of rupture can occur when parents become distracted by their own needs and their child feels abandoned without the parents' awareness of the child's experience.[9]

All this stirs the child's survival instincts. Since an infant is dependent totally upon the caretakers for survival, if the caretakers seem distracted and fail to interact with the child, the ruptured connection triggers anxiety, which becomes the background of the child's consciousness and the source of all his or her potential problems.

Anxiety is the painful neural sensation activated by the child when the child feels threatened. The threat arouses the fear that he or she may not survive. It is such a painful sensation that anxious children turn inward and becomes self-absorbed—in the pain—with tragic consequences.

Of course, these damaged children are not aware or even thinking about all this. But behind the scenes, their autonomic nervous systems are marshaling their defenses—flight, fight, freeze, or fawn—to protect themselves from the consequences of failed parenting.

Unless their relationships improve, as anxious children grow into adults they will continue to live in a self-constructed world while believing it is the objective world, the world outside. They will assume that all others share their worldview. When they find this is not true—that, in fact, others have views that are different from theirs—they make every effort to convince themselves and others that their worldview is the only correct one.

We call this problem "objection to difference." It's an illusory state in which some believe that their views of the world are the only valid views, and everyone else should accept them. As a result, they cannot see, much less accept, different opinions and perspectives that do not align with their own.

We believe this objection to difference is the source of conflict and polarization that produces all negative social behavior.

Now here is a fascinating paradox: objection to difference is a negative attempt to do something positive. The objectors try to convince others to adopt their point of view because they see their perspective as *the* truth that will benefit everyone if only they see it this way. However, by claiming that theirs is the only valid view, they turn those with opposing views into mere objects, and eventually, into opponents.

All humans want to experience connection with others because it is our nature. However, we often express our desire to connect in ways that drive people with different beliefs and perspectives away.

This is the tragic nature of being human.

Negative Connections

The doctor's rude response to Sarah is one example of someone trying to connect with another person by sharing their perspective. The doctor may have thought he had the patient's best interest at heart, but he failed to accept Sarah's differing view, which deepened the relational rupture between them. We call this a "negative connection."

You likely can come up with many of your own examples of negative connections based on daily experiences.

Here are a few common real-world scenarios:

1. A friend who is more liberal than you immediately dismisses your point of view because it conflicts with her own (or vice versa).
2. Rather than giving clear instructions to you, your boss assumes you know what is expected of you and then reacts negatively when you don't.
3. A family member guilts you when you won't come to their house for the holidays.
4. A friend interrupts you when you describe your feelings about the abortion issue because this person disagrees with you and wants you to hear what they are saying.
5. Your spouse repeatedly points out things you are doing wrong with the intention of improving you.

Most people agree with the old saying that "variety is the spice of life." (No, the spice of life is not turmeric, despite recent trends.) Yet perhaps because of our subconscious biases, differences of opinion can be upsetting and even threatening at times. Therefore we attempt to convince others to see it our way. Let's face it. When others don't see the world in the same way we see it, we can express frustration, annoyance, and maybe even outrage.

We may not be conscious of feeling threatened by their differing views because that is just the way our brains work when we experience anxiety. Those who cannot tolerate different points of view may simply march off and pout, or withdraw to their own fortresses of solitude, which is counterproductive, at least for those of us who are not superheroes. Or they may lash out in violence, which increasingly seems to be the case. This dangerous refusal to acknowledge differences can be seen as "the polarized mind."

Psychologists Kirk J. Schneider and Sayyed Mohsen Fatemi believe that "so much of what we call human depravity ('evil') seems to be based on a principle termed 'the polarized mind.' The polarized mind is the fixation on a single point of view to the utter exclusion of competing points of view, and it has caused more human torment and misery than virtually any other factor."[10]

Self-Absorption Leads to Polarization and Isolation

Self-absorption can lead to social isolation, which is not healthy for humans because we thrive on safe relationships with other humans. When we build walls because we can't bear to consider or even hear different opinions and perspectives, those walls might keep others out, but they also box us in, creating anxiety that produces depression and alienation.

Eventually, the throbbing pain from our bruised egos may subside, and we may dare to step back out from behind those walls. But unless we've abandoned our "I am obviously right, and you are obviously wrong," and "I accept no dissenting opinions" attitude, we likely will face the same anxiety and, as soon as anyone dares to suggest that our view is not the only one in the universe, we will turn anxiety into the more tolerable emotion of anger.

Remember, closed minds lead to closed hearts. You may be correct in your views, but, unfortunately, you live on a planet populated by other humans who are not placed on Earth to agree with you, validate your every opinion, and serve your purpose as their object—as nice as that might sound.

When you adopt the "my way or the highway" attitude, you not only lose support but also your compassion. With that, you also lose your humanity. This is the danger we mentioned earlier—that you may find yourself seeing other humans as mere objects, like potted plants serving as the scenery or props on your life stage. That point of view may soothe those who don't like differing opinions, but it is no way to win friends and influence people—and it's no way to live.

Not-So-Great Expectations

When George and Mary, married for two years, came for their therapy appointment, George started by reporting that they were having regular and intensive arguments about whether to have a child. He wanted to be a father. Mary came from a large and broken family. She had ambivalence about even being married and did not want to be a mother. She preferred to develop a career without the distraction of parenting.

As we turned them to face each other and talk about their situation, both reported that during their three years of courtship and cohabitation, neither had talked about their wishes about parenting, but Mary had studiously avoided getting pregnant. But when they married, George, who grew up in a relatively stable family with one brother, expected that Mary would naturally want a family of her own.

When he raised the issue, he was shocked by Mary's response and expressed his disappointment. Mary retaliated by reminding him that during their dating years, George had encouraged her to finish a degree and find employment she would love. She expected that he would understand that she'd had a challenging childhood and therefore wanted the freedom to pursue a career and financial independence.

Talking through their differences and the intensity of their opposing visions required many long and challenging conversations that eventually led to a collaborative compromise. They agreed to delay having children so that Mary could pursue her career. Then, before it was too late for her to conceive, they would discuss whether or not to have children.

In our early years of working with polarized and disconnected couples, we learned that all too often, their arguments and disagreements were rooted in the expectation that they would always see things in the same way, share the same views, and form the same opinions.

We learned that when those expectations were not met, couples struggled because they couldn't accept their differences. We also observed that couples, including ourselves, subconsciously had expectations and made assumptions about how our partners should behave.

In our case, Harville is a loner who likes to do things on his own because he was overcontrolled when he was young. He lived on a farm where everyone worked. If he wanted to read—which he still loves doing to this day—he had to hide in the loft of the barn.

For her part, Helen grew up in a complex family and did not feel visible to her very busy and frequently absent parents. As a result, when Harville opts for private time or wants to do things on his own, that triggers Helen's feelings of being excluded and invisible.

We may give lip service to American individuality and even shout, "Vive la différence!" from time to time. But when it comes to our relationships, we tend to wish for—and even expect—uniformity of perspective and opinions.

The advertising firm working for the Gatorade brand in the 1990s understood this basic human inclination when creating the memorable Be Like Mike campaign, featuring basketball-star-turned-legend Michael Jordan. That slogan was, in turn, inspired by the song "I Wan'na Be Like You" from *The Jungle Book* film by Disney, according to those involved.[11]

Now, "Be Different Than Mike" or "I Don't Wanna Be Like You" just don't have the same appeal as slogans or song lyrics, do they? That is because differences can be disappointing and frustrating, whether in a romantic relationship, a business environment, or social and organizational settings. Maybe this helps explain why so many older couples move into communities reserved for people their own age, like The Villages in Florida or Sun City developments across the country. Or why we tend to gravitate toward those who share our own political views, religious beliefs, and economic status.

As we began our work helping couples with their relationships, we found that even when they were willing to acknowledge that other perspectives existed, many felt anxious and threatened by differing views. They were compelled to reject or challenge their partner as a result.

There is also a tendency to dehumanize those with differing views by sticking labels on them. You see this name-calling and dehumanizing happening all around you these days, especially in clashes between political parties, religious groups, and those on opposite sides of the abortion issue. You can also see it between the most vehement supporters of competing sports teams and between businesses' employees and management.

Why Can't We All Just Get Along?

Why can't we all get along? seems to be the question of the decade, but it has been the challenge of the centuries. Our goal is to offer you some answers. One important point we will make is that we must recover the vision that while each of us is unique, we also are a part of the whole. Early in life, we experienced belonging and oneness, but for some it was ruptured and replaced with anxiety and a sense of separateness.

To experience our true natures, we must find ways to overcome divisiveness and polarization caused by self-absorption. We will show you how to create safe environments in which you can connect and accept difference. After all, isn't difference the primary feature of nature? In fact, since there is no such thing as "sameness," trying to annihilate difference is a delusion.

We acknowledge that creating a safe environment may not be an easy task, given how many times you have run into people who flat out reject any opinions or perspectives that don't agree with their own. It doesn't help either that many people don't even acknowledge that you are welcome to your own opinion. In fact, they may say you and your opinion are not welcome at all. But we are up to the challenge of helping you!

We want to emphasize that ruptured connections are usually the result of a monologue or parallel monologues, which hold that the differing views of others are unequal if not erroneous. This makes talking itself a dangerous undertaking and makes thoughtful listening impossible. Rejection of different views has existed throughout human existence as a divisive and destructive force. And it seems to have spread more widely in recent decades.

Or maybe our enhanced media sources are telling us more about what has always existed. Maybe social media is helping us become more aware of this psychic state in which individuals decide that if you don't agree with them, then you are no more than scenery in their lives—and unwelcome scenery at that.

In our work with individuals and their relationships, we have developed some theories as to why so many people are intolerant of differing viewpoints and in such need of validation for their own opinions. We believe there are three sources of these disconnections in our lives that can cause us to withdraw and assume that those who do not conform to our expectations simply do not matter.

1. The first is **unconscious caretaking**, which occurs when a caregiver is not emotionally bonded with a child during development. As a result, the child disconnects emotionally from the parent as well as other people. The more unattuned the caregiver is to the child, the more traumatic it is

for the little one. And, too often, the disconnect endures into adulthood.

2. The second source of disconnection in childhood comes from a **traumatic experience**—mild or intense—which might be a scare from an encounter with a pet, a humiliating experience in grade school, bullying from playmates, abuse by an adult, or simply a parent who turned away from you or displayed a cold "still face." Traumatic experiences like these create debilitating memories and often trigger distrust and self-isolation to avoid similar experiences.

3. The third source, as we noted earlier, is a disconnect caused by **the value system of our culture**. Our society promotes being the best and excelling throughout childhood, whether it is striving for the highest grades or being the most athletic or most attractive. Excelling and standing out becomes more important than connecting to other people on an emotional level, which can lead to narcissism and a sense that you are the center of the universe and everyone else is lucky to be in your orbit.

This cultural value system cited in the third source of disconnect historically has been encouraged by the mental-health field, which promotes the goal of moving from the dependency of childhood to autonomy, self-reliance, and independence as an adult, and a culture that rewards the "best." The problem with this value system is that we are relational beings. We can survive in an unsafe environment, but we thrive only when we have safe, healthy relationships; therefore, we should be taught to value them and our interdependence on one another.

The Effects of Disconnection

Psychologist Abraham Maslow's classic model for the hierarchy of human needs identified five categories, which are:

1. Physiological needs: These are essential for human survival, including food, clothing, water, and shelter.
2. Safety needs: We all need to feel secure and protected from harm.
3. Sense of belonging: We all want to feel loved and part of a community.
4. Esteem needs: Everyone wants to feel respected and appreciated.
5. Self-actualization: This makes us feel we have fulfilled our potential and are serving a purpose higher than ourselves.[12]

In looking at Maslow's hierarchy, you can see that anyone who feels disconnected emotionally from others is likely missing out on several of the basic human needs, including feeling heard, seen, and valued, and, thus, not experiencing safety and belonging.

Social isolation can trigger all sorts of undesirable psychological and emotional issues, including anxiety, loneliness, depression, and panic attacks. We also know that people who don't have healthy relationships, or even casual relationships, may become angry and lash out.

How often have you heard someone responsible for a mass shooting or other random act of violence described as a "lone wolf"? Or as someone who had few friends and was antisocial?

The same can often be said of people who symbiotically merge others' views into their minds and polarize by being intolerant of other opinions or viewpoints and are, thus, incapable of productive discussions and open-minded conversations.

Here are a few other characteristics we have identified in those who are disconnected and resentful of anyone whose perceptions differ from theirs.

ANXIETY

Phyllis and her lifelong friend Maria had so many things in common that they often felt like sisters, but there was one difference that eventually drove them apart. Phyllis believed that all women should stay at home so they could be good mothers and take care of their husbands and children. Maria thought that women should be free to choose a career and be economically equal to their husbands, even at the expense of having a family.

Even though they could have focused on the many other issues they agreed upon, Phyllis and Maria found themselves arguing about women's roles so much that they eventually stopped speaking to each other. The two women had supported each other through many challenging times over their decades of friendship. They had told each other things they would not tell anyone else. When they stopped speaking to each other, both became lonely and anxious.

The pain that emerges from lost connections in our lives can produce high levels of anxiety. The reason for this is that anxiety, unlike fear, is a general condition with no specific object of fear.

Fear is stimulated by a knock on the door in the night, a lion in your path, or a barking dog. Anxiety is triggered by imagining that behind a specific fear lies the possibility that we might cease to exist. This fear of not being at all is experienced as a neurological sensation that travels the nervous system of our bodies and underlies all specific fears.

This is so important that it bears repeating: *the sensation of anxiety is so painful that we cannot tolerate it.* Therefore, we convert it into a tolerable and empowering emotion—anger—so we can take action to protect ourselves. Or we succumb to the threat and collapse into depression and despair and give up trying. In either case, we insulate ourselves from the awareness of the possibility of nonbeing.

In all cases, we don't want to risk being hurt again, so we put up walls, which only makes us feel alienated and even more anxious. The only information we process is from our own thoughts, which are not positive or productive but only heighten our anxiousness. At this point, those who care about us may grow frustrated, telling us to "get over it." And the connection is ruptured again, making everything worse.

SELF-ABSORPTION

The pain of the anxiety triggered by ruptured connections produces a state of self-absorption. You probably know this if you have ever experienced a divorce, breakup, the loss of a friendship, being fired from a job, or alienation from a family member. If some version of that has happened, you have probably experienced degrees of anxiety ranging from mild to intense, and you may have gone through at least a brief period of withdrawal to grieve and self-soothe.

Since anxiety produces self-absorption, we often feel as though no one else has ever gone through what we are going through, which isn't true, of course, but seems true in the moment. At some point, when you have become self-absorbed, a friend or family member may say to you, "Do you think you're the only person who has gone through this?" Or, "You know, other people have even bigger problems to deal with." Or, "You need to get your head out of the sand and look around." Or something to that effect.

Imagine going to a beach where you are surrounded by miles of sand. The sky above you is beautiful, and the ocean in front of you has mesmerizing waves. You are relaxing, walking down the long, peaceful sandy beach, taking in the beauty of everything around you. But at one point, you step on a sharp rock under the sand that cuts your toe. Ouch! Your toe begins to bleed. The pain blinds you. Suddenly, there is no beach or tide or beauty around you. All pleasure and relaxed joyfulness disappear. The only reality is your hurting, bleeding toe. Once the pain subsides, you can once again enjoy the beauty around you. But your body remembers the incident, so you might be a bit more tense and careful walking on the beach in the future. This is a metaphor for experiencing a painful incident in childhood. You become a bit more anxious and cautious, especially if you are in a similar environment to the original experience that caused the rupture.

The interesting thing is that while you and I have the power to shut out all that is positive and empowering in our lives, we also have the power to welcome all that is good back into our lives, while relegating all that is bad to a distant corner of our consciousness.

LOSS OF EMPATHY

A young mother went to the nursery after she recovered from giving birth to her son and was disturbed that all the infants, including hers, were crying. When she asked what was wrong, the nurse explained to her that this tends to happen when one infant experiences some discomfort and cries out for attention. The other babies respond in resonance and will often cry until the distressed infant is comforted and stops.

Researchers interested in this phenomenon report that babies experience empathy when one of their infant colleagues is distressed. They call it *proto-empathy*, meaning it is not fully developed but evolves as the infants grow older—unless they experience conditions that stimulate their anxiety. Then the empathic response disappears, and the baby will cry only when *he* is distressed.[13]

Loss of empathy is the tragic casualty of self-absorption, that state of isolation we inhabit when we experience the anxiety of ruptured connections. Note: *empathy* is different from *sympathy*. A sympathetic response is an emotion—sadness, fear, excitement—triggered when someone tells you about their distress, and you respond that you understand exactly what they are experiencing because "that happened to me too."

In radical contrast, empathy is a response to someone who shares a painful or joyful experience you have never had, but you can experience their experience, or at least imagine it. In an empathic response, you peer into the feelings of another person. Your own experience is enlarged and enriched by absorbing and holding, without any criticism, the inner world of another person, even if only for a few minutes.

OBJECTIFICATION

Steven was a very successful car salesman early in his career, but over the years, he came to feel that his bosses did not appreciate him or his goals in life. Not feeling seen or valued, he applied to become the general manager of sales but was turned down. After that disappointment, Steven decided to simply focus on making as much money as he could.

But that approach did not work. His sales plummeted. Instead of listening to his customers and learning what their needs and desires were regarding a car, his only goal was to sell them the car that would earn him the highest commission. He stopped seeing customers as individuals with their own goals and expectations. He saw them only as means to his ends.

When we cannot experience or imagine the inner world or feelings of another person and value them, we lose our ability to see them as humans. We transform them into objects. Then we can do anything we want to them. They are valuable to us only when they are useful to us. Otherwise, they are of no interest.

The person who feels rejected and unloved tends to view others as objects to be used or ignored. By objectifying others, the alienated person cares nothing about their feelings or needs and loses all humanity as a result.

Those who objectify others, then, reject anyone who has a different view or perspective.

Self-absorption produced by anxiety shuts down our capacity for positive social engagement. We turn other people into objects to serve our selfish needs and help us reach our goals. The outside world is rejected in favor of our interior world, which becomes "the" world.

On a societal or national level, those who have no tolerance for different opinions or viewpoints tend to believe that their own culture, race, religion, or lifestyle is the "right" one. They believe that their view of the world is the only way to see it, and others with different views are worthless and evil. The "others" are no longer humans but objects and are treated as such.

The Desire for Reconnection

The problem with viewing others as objects is that by dehumanizing them, we lose our own humanity and our connection to those in the world around us. Yet most of us yearn for relationships that connect us to others. We spend much of our lives looking for ways to connect with people in our private lives, our work, and our communities. But those who have no tolerance for differing opinions and viewpoints end up frustrated and angry because they can't connect.

The good news is that in the following chapters, we offer a way to make connections with those whom you might otherwise find intolerable because your differences might serve as an insurmountable barrier or divide. The key to overcoming or transcending a resistance to differences is to accept that only "difference" exists. Every point of view is an example of difference. Difference is the fundamental feature of nature, and the goal is to become more understanding and tolerant of other perspectives. In our work with couples, corporate employees, schools, and religious communities, we call this "differentiation," which means listening to and valuing others by finding a secure way to relate to their uniqueness, even those with whom you may not agree.

Relationships constitute nature. All individual things arise out of an underlying oneness that is behind all diversity. And nature is dyadic; it is filled with opposites. Look at the colors that exist around you, the many flavors of food, the range of life-changing inventions, and the varieties of music. The universe is defined by difference. For every hot, there is a cold. For every up, there is a down. For every wet, there is a dry. For every loud, there is a quiet. Nature is filled with differences and polarities.

The goal is to be curious about those who may differ from

you with the aim of learning about other viewpoints and maybe even collaborating to find a consensus and cocreate an outcome that is a win-win for everyone. Or to develop an acceptance of the person with whom you disagree and a respect for the disagreement. After all, everyone is trying to do something good, from their perspective, including you. So a little compassion and validation are in order.

If you want to be part of this world, you must learn to listen to and value others by becoming curious and being respectful of differences. If you want to grow beyond the provincialism of your own mind, you have to accept diversity as a reality of nature and society. Otherwise, you will live in a world that is limited to the recycling of your own thoughts and the illusion that your own thoughts are reality.

The process we offer in this book is your path to improving interactions and building better relationships in your personal, professional, and community life, as well as becoming a part of global humanity. We will help you discover that the world consists *only* of difference and diversity, and we will demonstrate how accepting and honoring difference and diversity will open the door to greater opportunities and a happier life.

By using the method we teach in this book, you will learn how to communicate in a way that goes beyond differences, while allowing people with differing opinions and views to stay connected and productive.

CHAPTER 2

The Solution

Back in the early 1990s, in the early days of our Institute for Imago Relationship Therapy, we had some growing pains. Thanks to all the exposure we were receiving from *The Oprah Winfrey Show*, our staff was inundated with phone calls requesting workshops, therapists, and products.

We had not anticipated this massive increase in demand for our services and products. We scrambled to hire more staff, and at the same time, we incurred more costs for printing and mailing material to those requesting it. To help cover our growing costs, we instituted an annual fee for our Imago therapists, which included benefits such as being listed in our directory and marketing Imago for their practices.

The new fee was announced just before we held our annual conference and was not warmly received by our therapists. When the conference in Orlando convened, the initial mood was contentious. Many of them let us know that they were not happy about the additional charge and the way it was communicated. We took a lot of heat.

Maya Kollman, a dear friend of ours and an Imago Master Trainer, recalls that Harville vented his frustrations at the criticism.

We will step back and let Maya tell you the rest of the story:

I thought the whole organization was going to dissolve. On the last day, I was sitting at a table next to the microphone. I felt distressed, demoralized, and powerless to do anything about this conflict. Harville stood up on stage and wisely said, "Somebody mirror me!" I stepped up to the microphone and mirrored everything he had to say. The entire group was glued to us onstage. Harville was in a reactive mode, as he felt attacked during the conference.

So I mirrored him. "So you're really distressed. You feel like you've given so much. And it feels like people are ungrateful."

The more I mirrored Harville, the softer he became. And when I validated his feelings, he became tearful. My validation was: "It really makes sense that you've put your heart and soul into this organization, and hearing complaints is difficult and painful. And [moving into empathy] I imagine you might feel misunderstood, hurt, and disappointed."

By the end of our dialogue, the feeling in the room had completely changed. There were many tears. We were once again able to understand each other's different points of view and move to a collaborative working relationship.

I came away feeling that it was a healing experience for everyone. We all realized that people were upset about the new charges mostly because of the authoritarian way in which they were announced. The real issue was poor communication.

As Maya's story illustrates, "how" we talk, more than "what" we say, creates communication issues that can cause breakdowns in relationships that detract from the quality of our lives and our work. This is a prime example of vertical talking, which we call *monologue*, and the calming effect of a lateral way of talking, which we call *dialogue*. When we are willing to talk through differences and the tensions they have caused in a way that connects rather than polarizes, the relationship can be repaired, and the connection restored. Seeing, listening, and valuing will do it every time. If you are feeling disconnected from people in your personal or professional relationships, you may want to experiment with this process, which we will elaborate on later.

One major cause of fractured relationships and social disconnection is polarization, due to an objection to difference—opinion, race, gender, religion, politics. You name it. But here is the reality that we all face: *difference is the primary feature of everything in nature.* The universe is defined by difference. From the smallest particle to the largest galaxy, nothing in nature is the "same." Every "thing" is unique.

If you want to find a measure of peace and be helpful in this world, you must learn to become curious and respectful of differences. If you want to be a constructive member of society, you must come to terms with that reality and find a way to deal with it. In this chapter, we offer you a way to not only live with but to transcend differences—in whatever form you find them—so that you can build stronger relationships in your personal, professional, and social lives.

Here is a little comfort for the journey to the discovery and acceptance of "otherness": it is not all your fault, and we are all in this together. The key to transcending resistance to differences is to understand three things:

1. **How your brain works.** Although your brain is like other human brains in how it is organized and how it works, it is unique in *what* it knows and *what* it thinks about.

2. **The uniqueness of each human brain is a result of our personal histories, starting in childhood.** We each learn to "see" things a certain way. That holds true for everyone. Other people cannot naturally see things through our eyes because their personal histories have shaped how they see things. So we all have this problem. We are locked inside our brains with our personal views of the world, which we think everyone shares, and if they do not, we think they should.

3. **You can change your brain by being more curious about others.** Curiosity can be considered the royal road to self-transcendence and experiencing connecting with others. By opening your mind to learn how others see the world and why, and by accepting another perspective, you gain access to diverse viewpoints that will expand your own perspective on reality and improve your relationships with others. Your brain will change in a positive way, but not without curiosity.

Again, we call this *differentiation*, which is the ability to see, hear, and value the perspectives of others, even those with whom you may not agree. Furthermore, it means to accept that others are challenged, as you are, by this process when you share your perspective with them.

The goal is to create a new state of consciousness and awareness by accepting the fact that we are not alike and, apparently, are not meant to be. How boring would that be anyway? We are all unique, with our own opinions, viewpoints, perceptions, dreams, and desires. Instead of expecting and even demanding that your family, friends, coworkers, and social acquaintances all feel and think the same way as you do, you will find it much easier and more fulfilling to treat them respectfully and to try to understand them instead of "fix" them. That will save you a lot of effort and make life more interesting.

Jewish philosopher Martin Buber, author of the influential book *I and Thou*, said that most of us have "I–It" relationships in which we tend to see other people in transactional terms, like tools to be used for our own purposes. By approaching relationships as transformational rather than transactional, we can move into the "I–Thou" mode in which we feel mutual respect and want to invest in one another's success and happiness through collaboration and cooperation.[1]

We invite you to adopt an open-minded curiosity about those who may differ from you. When you are open to learning about other viewpoints, you are more likely to find common—but not the same—ground, or you can agree to disagree in a way that allows you to still have conversations and healthy relationships despite your differences. And you can keep your own point of view. You just have to allow others to do the same. In doing this, you will be able to shift from an I–It to an I–Thou relationship, which is more productive and fulfilling.

The process we offer is your path to improving interactions and building better relationships in your personal, professional, and community life. We will help you discover and celebrate a world of difference and diversity that will make your life interesting rather than scary. Honoring difference and diversity will open the door to greater opportunities and a happier life.

Safe Conversations Skills

We first developed our SC Dialogue skills for couples like us. We are strong-willed, independent thinkers who, quite naturally, do not always share the same opinions or perspectives. We enjoy our differences—most of the time—because we learn from each other. Still, we can clash like a couple of jousting knights over our differences, so we needed a method for connecting safely during those clashes—one that did not involve lances, axes, or broadswords—so we could communicate effectively. War horses and heavy armor were also not on the Safe Conversations tool list.

While working with thousands of couples in our workshops and therapy sessions over the years, we have refined our relationship-building methods. Our goal is to describe a way to practice dialogue so everyone can have a safe way to communicate and build relationships, despite differences, in the wider world of family and friends, coworkers, supervisors, customers, clients, shareholders, and others within your inner and outer circles of acquaintances and contacts.

Our SC Dialogue is a skill that provides a relatively simple road map to de-weaponize and disarm even today's most potentially volatile conversations, and to help transform any relationship from conflict to connecting so that you and those around you feel safer, more relaxed, and open to different points of view.

With our dialogue tools, you learn to:

- talk without criticism,
- listen with curiosity and without judgment, and
- connect beyond your differences.

One of our goals is to dispel the myth that you must simply surrender and walk away if you are having a relationship conflict with anyone with whom you want to get along—for professional or personal reasons. There is no need to ghost someone over a disagreement. We suggest you stick around for a more productive conversation by learning to see conflict not as a threat or as a fight-or-flight trigger, but as "growth trying to happen."

Conflict arises because differences arise, which, again, is a natural and even desirable fact of life. Differences, after all, are how we evolve genetically and intellectually. If you decide to embrace conflict as a path to growth, you are safe to unleash your curiosity rather than being angered or intimidated by different viewpoints. Instead, you and your cocombatants can look forward to discovering paths to understanding each other that will leave you both more fulfilled, wiser, and emotionally healthier.

Once again, we encourage you to put down your dukes and stand your ground. Cheer out, "Vive la différence!" Put your differences into production. Use your curiosity to understand them. Make them work for you and for the betterment of your life and the lives of everyone around you. We can learn to celebrate diverse opinions and to live in a more collaborative, relatable way. Wouldn't you rather grow than go? We want you to learn *from* others and then learn to live *with* them as compassionate, loving human beings.

The Four Skills of Safe Conversations

Finding a pathway to be seen, heard, and valued and to see, hear, and value others involves learning and practicing four skills:

1. Safe Conversations Dialogue
2. Empathy with everyone
3. Zero negativity
4. Affirmations

PRACTICE SAFE CONVERSATIONS DIALOGUE

Consider Maya's story at the beginning of this chapter. When she observed me (Harville) going off the rails and venting my frustrations, she stepped in and turned my monologue into a dialogue, didn't she? She played listener to my speaker and then guided our conversation into a safer, nonconfrontational exchange that eventually resulted in connecting, rather than dissension and hard feelings.

Maya did this so skillfully that someone without training might not have recognized she was creating a dialogue through a three-step process: mirroring, validating, and empathizing. The three-step process allows opposing sides to feel seen, heard, and valued, despite their differences. They shift from judgment to curiosity about each other's views. Showing curiosity instead of animosity makes connections possible and clears the way for mutual understanding and maybe even peaceful collaboration—and gives you a better brain.

PRACTICE EMPATHY

Empathy can be a force for healing and understanding. When you use this tool to create a safe place for communication, you may find keys that explain the other person's perspective and actions, even if your differences remain. We all come from unique backgrounds and experiences that help forge our characters. So it helps to get some perspective on how the other people in your life developed such different views than you. By showing curiosity and listening to their stories, you may find where their paths diverged from yours—and also where your paths were similar. You can also be more aware that when you react negatively to another person, you may be unconsciously reliving a childhood memory that is affecting you in the moment.

PRACTICE ZERO NEGATIVITY

How do you think things would have gone at our conference if Maya had scolded Harville and told him to shut up and sit down instead of stepping up to engage him in a dialogue? If she'd used that negative approach, the result might have been more like throwing a burning match on a puddle of gasoline. You might think, *Well, I have to be honest about my differences of opinion. I can't sweep them under the rug.* We agree!

How do we define *negativity*? It's very simple. If the other person thinks it is negative, it is negative whether or not you meant it as a negative. When someone reports having a negative experience, it is called a *put-down* because they feel their status has somehow been diminished. If someone reports that you caused it to happen to them, it is important to immediately restore their sense of well-being.

PRACTICE AFFIRMATIONS

Have you ever had the experience of feeling "used" because you were valued only when you did what someone wanted you to do? Only when you complied would you be thanked; otherwise, you would be ignored. Or have you ever thought someone valued you only if you somehow served their purpose?

This internal monologue is very common. A more rare monologue is to value someone who is of "no value" to you, and to have no expectations that ultimately they will do something that is of value.

We learned that it was not enough to be compassionate and avoid negativity. It was important to add something that was positive. But our sources did not mean just "being positive" as an attitude. They wanted the positive expressed as a behavior.

The magic of the Safe Conversations process is that you feel *safe*; therefore, you can talk and listen with mutual respect. We see it as an efficient communication tool for the exchange of energy and information because all participants are seen, heard, and valued. With this structure, safety happens; when safety happens, connecting happens. And connecting ignites a collaborative process that can transform the negative energy of conflict into the vibrant energy of feeling fulfilled and fully engaged in life so we can experience joyful aliveness—our original state.

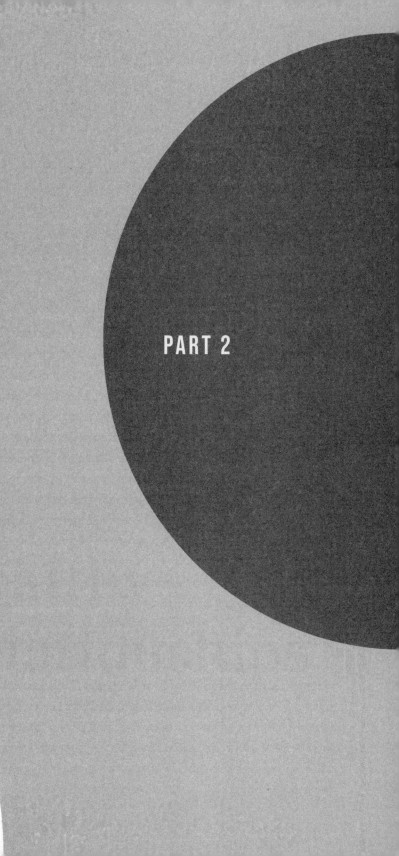

PART 2

CHAPTER 3

A Structured Dialogue

The following dialogue represents a typical political conversation in recent years:

> **Joe:** I think the candidate you're backing is a moron who will destroy our country.
> **Charlie:** Well, I think you're a moron, and the candidate you're backing isn't fit to lead a one-man garbage crew.
> **Joe:** You're an idiot!
> **Charlie:** And you're really, really stupid!

And here is our suggested new-and-improved model:

> **Joe:** I'd like to hear more about the candidate you're supporting. What do you see as his strong points?
> **Charlie:** You're really interested in the candidate I'd like to see elected?
> **Joe:** Look, we've been friends for a long time, and I

      respect you. So I want to understand why you're
      supporting this guy.

Charlie: Well, if you sincerely mean that, let's meet for
      coffee. Maybe we can learn something from each
      other, even if we agree to disagree in the end.

We think you and the rest of the world have had enough of combative conversations. Wouldn't it be nice to enjoy talking without criticism, listening without judgment, and connecting beyond difference?

SC Dialogue is our new way of conversing that does just that for you. It is a skill that ensures you are seen, heard, and valued. Upon mastering this method, people with differing opinions and viewpoints can experience safety and connecting. They can communicate beyond their differences. It is a simple skill that, with practice, improves all forms of communication—sharing experiences and appreciations, and expressing frustrations and fears. This puts two or more parties "on the same page."

This new way to communicate involves deep listening with curiosity and empathy. Being curious when listening—rather than judgmental—creates greater safety between people, helping them experience connection rather than hostility and polarization.

Our ambition is to transform the world with our peace-seeking structured dialogue skills. Call us over-the-top optimists, but we think humanity is ready for more thoughtful and productive conversations. Our goal, then, is to launch a global social movement to introduce 2.5 billion people (the tipping point—25 percent—of the world's projected population in 2050) to our three-step process that helps people change *how* they have conversations, not *what* they talk about, so they can talk with anyone about anything without becoming contentious and polarized.

Instead, they can create deep and abiding connections, one conversation at a time.

Changing the world is a heavy load to lay on conversation alone. So let's take a look at what a dialogic conversation is. It's actually very simple. A dialogic conversation is talking *with* rather than talking *to* someone in a monologue.

Monologues are fine if you are watching a late-night talk show host deliver funny comments, or an actor delivering lines, but nobody wants to be talked *at* in conversations. You have no doubt had the experience of thinking you are in a conversation and then realizing, no, the other person is delivering a monologue and has no interest in hearing anything you might have to say. On the other hand, you might need to consider that the person talking with no interest in listening might be you!

Have you ever felt as though someone was just spewing their views for their own entertainment, and your presence wasn't really a factor? Monologues often seem insensitive and even oppressive. The monologuist usually comes off as patronizing and condescending, with an air of superiority, which tends to shut down conversational engagement. Monologuists drive us apart instead of bringing us together. As a result, listeners feel invisible, unheard, devalued, and unequal. This makes talking a dangerous activity, even more so these days.

Making Conversations More Constructive and Less Confrontational

In a world where so many conversations lead to combat, or nowhere at all, we are sending SC Dialogue to the rescue. While our solution may be understood as a better way to communicate, it is far more than that. This is an entirely new way to relate to others.

Let us dare to make a pop culture reference—our goal is to do for conversation what Justin Timberlake (or at least his song) did for *sexy*. We want to bring constructive conversation back! How? Through productive discussions, enlightening conversations, harmonious debates, conflict-free negotiations, and conflict resolution. Only then can we end violence and facilitate peace on earth. That's all! We know this is a big goal, but isn't that our collective human dream?

We believe that if SC Dialogue was embraced by 25 percent of the world's population, it would replace our individualistic civilization that focuses on the self and values competition, control, and a winner-takes-all mindset. In its place, we want to see a civilization based on relationships that would support a new set of values that include total personal freedom; social, economic, religious, and political equality for everyone; plus radical inclusion and the celebration of diversity.

What a world that would be!

Our SC Dialogue skill creates a context in which no one involved is trying to change, control, or overpower anyone else. Instead, the goal is to see, hear, and value one another. At the basic level, SC Dialogue is two or more people taking turns, talking without judging, listening without criticizing, and connecting beyond differences.

Now let's take a look at how to implement SC Dialogue. While its use promotes emotional and mental well-being, it is not a form of therapy. But it can be very therapeutic because it helps us build healthy relationships even though we might have areas of disagreement. Healthy relationships promote emotional and mental well-being.

As we elaborate on SC Dialogue, we will talk about the Space-Between, which we define as an energy field that exists between two or more people when they are interacting. Our dialogue transforms the Space-Between into a safe place instead of a battleground, allowing us to relax, experience connection, and embody relaxed joyfulness.

At the deepest level, Safe Conversations move us away from transactional communication, which involves making deals, to transformational connecting, which involves giving without asking for something back. Polarization is replaced with collaboration. This moves you to the next and higher level of relating, and eventually, when a tipping point is reached, to the next stage of civilization.

The Basics of SC Dialogue

SC Dialogue is a skill that consists of a speaker and listener following a three-step process:

1. **Mirroring:** the listener accurately reflects back what they heard the speaker say.
2. **Validating:** the listener sees the truth of the speaker's point of view while retaining their own.
3. **Empathizing:** the listener accurately shares their experience and/or imagining of the speaker's emotions as they are experiencing their world.

This structure is the royal road to mutuality in being seen, heard, and valued. With structure, safety happens; when safety happens, connecting happens. When connecting occurs, a cocreative process is ignited that transforms the negative energy of conflict into the vibrant energy of full aliveness and the relaxed energy of joyfulness.

SC Dialogue begins with mastery of the structure and then moves into spontaneity, which is like a musician moving from practicing the skills of reading music into a natural flow so that the musician is no longer thinking about what to do but instead *just doing it.*

Our dialogue skill uses "sentence stems" to facilitate the three-step process. These consist of a sentence followed by a blank to be filled in by the speaker. Each sentence stem is designed to:

- create safety through predictability and structure;
- regulate emotion by keeping the focus on the topic;
- prevent negativity and polarization;
- regulate interaction between thinking and feeling, which is essential for sustaining changes;
- deepen access to unspoken feelings and thoughts or forgotten memories;
- deepen the connection between speaker and listener; and
- relax the defenses and replace reacting with intentional, focused responding.

Setting Up the Appointment

Honoring boundaries is essential in all relationships. Yet we often assume that other people are available twenty-four seven and, thus, jump right into sharing (a frustration, an appreciation, a request, and so on). Therefore, the appointment process is a crucial first skill in the SC Dialogue method because it recognizes the importance of boundaries.

The "appointment-only rule" insists that you share anything (stories, thoughts, feelings) by *appointment only*. Appointments for dialogue invite listeners to be fully available to listen, and help speakers develop the necessary muscle to be more intentional in their communication. Making an appointment starts with this sentence stem: "Is now a good time to talk about [*state the topic*]?" Examples include:

Is now a good time to talk about

. . . today's meeting?
. . . your report card?
. . . Dad's declining health?
. . . a concern I have about finances?
. . . an appreciation I have for you?

The listener should respond by saying, "Yes, I am available now." If they are not available, the listener is free to decline momentarily, but they need to offer a time when they will be available within twenty-four hours: "I'm not available at the moment but can be in an hour."

Requesting an appointment might feel awkward initially, but there are several reasons for making an appointment.

- **Honoring boundaries:** Because we are self-absorbed, we tend to assume the other person is available to us twenty-four seven. The appointment-only rule breaks this illusion and begins to see the other as an "other" and not as an extension of oneself. In our observations, boundary violations are the source of most conflict, including war.

- **Containing energy:** Some people tend to launch into a monologue, with predictable results. Asking for an appointment strengthens the intentionality and containment muscles.
- **Assuring emotionally availability:** Often, we are physically present but emotionally absent or mentally distracted. An appointment allows the listener to be fully available and present in the here and now without competing distractions.

When the appointment time is agreed upon, we encourage both the speaker and the listener to make eye contact and take three deep breaths in sync.

Eye contact contributes to the quality of the exchange of words. This is important because the brain interprets the size of others' pupils. When the brain sees large pupils, it interprets the other as "open" and "safe" and relaxes its defenses. If their pupils are small, the brain interprets them as "closed" and "dangerous," which activates their defenses.[1]

Open pupils facilitate sharing vulnerable feelings and thoughts; small pupils call for caution and monitored sharing. If both the speaker and the listener make eye contact and breathe in sync, their brains will be flooded with oxygen, which will enlarge their pupils and lower their blood pressure. Both people then begin to feel safer, and the words they exchange will contribute to connecting rather than polarizing.

Step One: Mirroring

Now that the setup is complete, you can proceed to the first step of SC Dialogue, which is mirroring—the act of accurately reflecting back the content, tone, and intensity of the speaker's message with as much thoughtfulness and sensitivity as possible and without adding to or emphasizing anything. The listener can either use "word for word" or a paraphrase of what the speaker said. It's the speaker's choice. The listener should mirror in the way the speaker feels most heard.

Mirroring requires not only that the listener practice the skill of word-for-word reflection or paraphrasing, but also that both the speaker and the listener take on a special attitude, one characterized by intentionality and goodwill. This is harder than it sounds. It requires mirroring messages that might, to the listener, seem unimportant, illogical, or otherwise at odds with the listener's perspective, triggering their objection to difference.

What many of us have never experienced, yet long for, is to see our own being reflected in the eyes of another. Hearing your own message mirrored back to you accurately and completely, with all its emotional overtones included, gives you the impression that the listener is really there and hearing what you're saying.

By mirroring each other, the speaker receives the message that they are inherently worthy, valuable, and lovable. That's what we all want: to be seen and heard and valued.

Mirroring is simple, but it's not easy—especially when partners are discussing emotional topics. Let's return to Joe and Charlie, who we started with at the beginning of this chapter.

Lifelong friends since grade school, Joe and Charlie found themselves on opposite sides of the political spectrum. Historically, this was never an issue in their friendship as they frequently took playful jabs at each other, such as "Commie liberal" and "racist white dude." But those jokes began waning as the political differences became more pronounced and belligerent in the public arena. For a while, Joe and Charlie would just "not go there." Until they did.

> **Joe:** I think the candidate you're backing is a moron who will destroy our country.
>
> **Charlie:** Well, I think you're a moron, and the candidate you're backing isn't fit to lead a one-man garbage crew.
>
> **Joe:** You're an idiot!
>
> **Charlie:** And you're really, really stupid!

At this point, the possibility of negative escalation leading to the end of a lifelong friendship was real. Both made the Space-Between a zone of negativity with personal attacks, something from which it is hard to recover. Now let's demonstrate how a reactive monologue can get short-circuited by a single brilliantly timed instance of mirroring.

What if, instead of responding to Joe's comment, Charlie mirrored him?

> **Joe:** I think the candidate you're backing is a moron who will destroy our country.
>
> **Charlie:** If I heard you correctly, you think the candidate I'm backing is a moron who will destroy our country. Did I get that?

How do you think Joe would respond to Charlie's mirroring? Most likely, after closing his mouth that was agape with shock, Joe would move into a less defensive response with something like this: "Yes, you got that! Sorry, that was a bit attacking. I know we have differing views on this. And I really do value your opinion. Are you available to discuss this further over coffee?"

Mirroring is the calming response that turns down the heat of anger.

FINE-TUNING THE MIRRORING

Along with repeating the cycle of sending, receiving, and mirroring, SC Dialogue includes more subtle substeps that help to enhance the impact of mirroring, which ultimately strengthens the dialogue. These include invitation statements made by the listener after mirroring, such as: *Did I get it?* and *Did I hear you accurately?*

This sentence stem is called an "accuracy check." Since our brains so easily fall prey to our own inner chatter, this accuracy check increases our ability to focus on each other. For many people, when they start the SC Dialogue process, they discover that they are not very good listeners. The accuracy check ensures the message heard was indeed the message sent.

After the accuracy check, another powerful follow-up is to become curious, using the following sentence stem: *Is there more about that?*

This question conveys that the listener is not only listening but is also curious about what the other person is experiencing and wants to hear more. This curiosity also deepens the speaker's sense of safety in the conversation. That sense of safety invites the speaker to express more and to go deeper. This is the golden mean of SC Dialogue. Simultaneously, the listener benefits from hearing more because they gain additional information to better understand the speaker's viewpoint.

After there is "no more," and after the accuracy check, the

listener can offer a paraphrased summary of everything they heard. The sentence stem goes like this: *Let me see if I got everything you said. If I did, you said* _____. *Did I get it all?*

SC Dialogue Step 1: Mirroring

After the speaker speaks, the listener:

1. Mirrors: "If I got that, you are saying ..." or "You are saying that ..."
2. Checks on the accuracy of the mirroring: "Did I get it?"
3. Expresses curiosity by asking: "Is there more about that?"
4. Summarizes the speaker's entire message: "If I got all of that, you said ..."
5. Checks for accuracy again: "Did I get it all?"

THE CHALLENGES AND BENEFITS OF MIRRORING

In some dialogues, the listener may have difficulty understanding the speaker's message. There are at least a couple of reasons why this might happen:

1. The listener has not received enough information to understand the speaker's perspective, and they cannot mirror what they do not yet understand.
2. The listener is having difficulty putting aside their own thoughts and feelings enough to make a clear space to understand the speaker's message.

In either case, the solution is the same: the speaker needs to say more, with the listener continuing to mirror, until the speaker's message is clear to the listener—enough so that they can accurately mirror the speaker's words.

Although it may seem simple, hearing and repeating back accurately—without distortion or additions—can be very challenging for partners. It's a muscle that is weak for most of us and can be a mentally and emotionally demanding task. Mirroring is training for quieting the inner mind (that is, reactivity) and hearing the pure voice of another. Mirroring requires a lot from the listener, including:

- focused attention and concentration,
- emotional availability and attunement,
- suspending criticism and judgment while engaging their curiosity,
- the willingness to temporarily suspend their own perspective to fully consider the viewpoint of their partner,
- accepting the fact that their partner experiences some things differently than them, and
- the ability to regulate their own emotional reactions and responses, both verbal and nonverbal, until it's their turn to speak.

Mirroring is also difficult because it is extremely hard—if not impossible—to give to another what we rarely receive. But we can learn how to. We have witnessed the profound effect of the simple act of mirroring on both the speaker and the listener. We have seen people who have never experienced what it feels like to be listened to so deeply break down in tears because they felt so profoundly moved by the experience. A phrase we often say is, "Without an echo, the voice dies."

Mirroring satisfies part of the human longing to experience being seen, heard, and valued, and connecting with others. At any age, when one person mirrors another, it communicates, "You matter. I care enough to listen to you, to really get you." It also sends a message: "I am no longer the sole person in the universe. I am acknowledging your separate existence. Your thoughts are important to me."

Step Two: Validation

Validation is the second step of an SC Dialogue. *Validation* is when we make somebody feel valued as a person or acknowledge that their ideas or opinions are worthwhile. Very simply, it sends a message from the listener to the speaker: "You make sense."

Validation requires listeners to suspend their personal truths for a moment and to see the speaker's version of the truth. This does not mean you have to agree or surrender your own viewpoint. It simply means that two versions of truth can occupy the same space.

In our experience, validation seems to be the most demanding step of our SC Dialogue process for many people. Yet it may be the most important step of all, and here's why: being validated—receiving the explicit message that what we are experiencing makes sense to another—is precisely the opposite of what many of us experience much of the time.

Too many of us, especially when it comes to hot-topic issues, are afraid that if we see the sense in another's experience, it means we are giving up our own opinion. How often have you heard one person say to another, "You're crazy!" or "You shouldn't feel that way," or "That makes no sense"?

If you've ever been on the receiving end of an invalidating statement, how did it make you feel? Did it encourage you to share more of your thoughts and feelings and continue engaging in conversations? Or did it cause you to withdraw, retreat, and shut down?

We all have unique perceptions of what is true. Pure agreement isn't possible given that we are all different and unique in so many ways. Validation prepares us to see others' perceptions as equal to our own.

With validation, we enter our dialogue partner's mental sanctum to see what lies within and to articulate to the other person two things: 1) that their experience makes sense to us (*"What you're saying makes sense"*), and 2) why it makes sense to us (*"What makes sense about it is _____"*).

Let's revisit Joe and Charlie's conversation about why they support their candidates. Charlie and Joe meet over coffee. After the setup process (asking for an appointment, making eye contact, and taking three deep breaths in sync), and before starting the topic at hand, the speaker sends an appreciation to the listener, which primes the Space-Between with safety.

> **Charlie:** I really value our friendship. We've been through a lot together and I consider you my best friend.

Now the listener simply mirrors, checks for accuracy, and shows gratitude for the appreciation.

> **Joe:** If I hear you correctly, you really appreciate our friendship. We've been through a lot together, and you consider me your best friend. Did I get that?

Charlie: Yes, you got that.

Joe: Thank you for sharing that appreciation with me.

Charlie then begins to share why he supports a particular candidate using "I" statements, devoid of any shame, blame, or criticism. After sharing his appreciation, Joe invites Charlie to share why he supports a particular candidate using "I" messages, devoid of any shame, blame, or criticism.

> **Charlie:** One reason why I support this particular candidate is because I feel he will address the illegal immigration problem in this country.

Note: Charlie uses "I" messages and expresses his opinion without knocking down Joe or the political opponent. He also picks only one topic—illegal immigration.

> **Joe:** Let me see if I got that. You support this candidate because you are concerned about illegal immigration and feel that your candidate will address this concern. Did I get that?
>
> **Charlie:** Yes, you got that.
>
> **Joe:** Is there more about that?
>
> **Charlie:** Yes, there's more. My candidate has been really vocal about the issue and, if elected, would make it his priority in his first hundred days in office. And I'm concerned about illegal immigration. It's not that I don't sympathize with people looking for a better life. But I fear an economic drain on our country. I mean, we can't even take care of our own citizens.

Joe would continue mirroring, checking for accuracy, and asking for more. Often, another sentence stem that helps move speakers during the mirroring phase is, "That feeling of _____ reminds me of _____."

When emotions are intense and repetitive, there is often an underlying memory connected to the experience. Bringing up a memory may not be appropriate for certain situations, such as in a meeting among board members. But with friends or partners, it fast-tracks understanding the sense and emotions underneath the experience.

> **Charlie:** This fear of an economic drain in our country reminds me of growing up with financial insecurity, never knowing if we were going to be forced to move again or if the electricity was going to be turned off.

The mirroring, accuracy check, and asking for more continues until there is "no more" about this topic. Next, Joe *summarizes* Charlie's message before moving into the validation step.

> **Joe:** Let me see if I got everything you're saying. One reason you support your candidate is because you feel he has a strong stance on illegal immigration. And one reason you're really concerned about immigration is because you feel it drains our country's economic resources. It's not that you're unsympathetic about the plight of others who are less fortunate. But you feel that our country can't even take care of its own citizens. And that fear of being an economic drain on our country reminds

you of growing up with financial insecurity and
never knowing if your family was going to have
to move again or if the electricity was going
to be turned off. Did I get that? Is that a good
summary?

Charlie: Yeah, that's it. You got it.

Now Joe makes a validation statement.

Joe: Well, that makes a lot of sense, Charlie. It makes
sense that you worry about illegal immigration
being a strain on our economy—especially when
you see that our country can't even support its
own citizens properly. And it would make sense
that the fear around finances would remind you
of growing up with financial insecurity. And it
makes sense that you would see your candidate as
strong to work with Congress to address this crisis
given his vocal views on the subject. Did I get that
right?

Charlie: Yeah, that really hits the bullseye! And I never
connected that fear of financial insecurity with my
past.

Validation truly is a gift from the listener to the speaker. The
experience of validation begins the process of reversing the messages we received throughout our lifetime (from parents, teachers,
employers, friends, strangers) that culminated in the impression
that we were wrong to feel what we felt or to want what we
wanted. But validation is just as much a gift for the one giving it
as it is for the listener.

> ## SC Dialogue Step 2: Validation
>
> After the speaker confirms the accuracy of the listener's summary, the listener makes a validation statement:
>
> "What you're saying makes sense to me, and what makes sense about it is..."
>
> "You make sense. I can see that you think _____ because _____."

THE CHALLENGES AND BENEFITS OF VALIDATION

Validating the other person in a conversation can be the most demanding step of SC Dialogue. Most of us are so ingrained in the belief that "the world is the way I see it!" that we cannot imagine, much less accept, that another point of view is as valid as our own. It is connected to our fear of the loss of self—*If I agree with you and it stands against my truth, then perhaps I don't exist or I am not valid.*

But again, validation is not agreement. The goal is to help you and the other person discover what distinguishes you from each other and to accept difference without judgment, since difference is reality. The goal is to see another person as they are, not as you wish them to be.

If a listener is unable to see the sense of the speaker's perspective, we encourage them to stay in the process and continue asking for more information. It is also why we encourage people to start with simple, noncontentious topics to practice so that the listening and containment muscles grow stronger.

The feeling of validation reverses the negative messages we tell ourselves based on past experiences that left us with the impression that we were wrong to feel what we felt, wrong to want what we wanted, or wrong to think what we thought.

On the other hand, validation is also a gift for the one providing it. The validator is freed to express curiosity about a world they may have never known and is invited to relinquish the belief that there is only one right way to see things. Validation also sets the stage for the last step of an SC Dialogue: empathy.

Step Three: Empathy

Mirroring aims to accurately reflect the content of the speaker's message. Validating is about seeing and understanding the "truth" of the speaker's experience. The third step of the SC Dialogue, empathy, is an exercise in experiencing how others feel, walking a mile in their moccasins, imagining what their world feels like in their experience. Empathy is being attuned to the emotions the other person is experiencing or, if the emotions are not overt, listening for feelings guiding their words.

Typically, empathy comes immediately after validation. To illustrate, let us briefly return once again to friends Joe and Charlie.

Joe: Well, that makes a lot of sense, Charlie. It makes sense that you worry about illegal immigration being a strain on our economy, especially when you see that our country can't even support its own citizens properly. And it would make sense that the fear around finances would remind you of growing up with financial insecurity. And it makes sense that you would see your candidate as strong to work with Congress to address this crisis given his vocal views on the subject. Did I get that right?

Charlie: Yeah, that really hits the bullseye! And I never connected that fear of financial insecurity with my past.

Next, Joe moves into the third step: empathy.

Joe: I can imagine, then, that you feel concerned and fearful for the country.

(Joe next checks on the accuracy of his empathy statement.)

Joe: Did I get those feelings right?

Charlie: Well, not exactly.

Joe: Will you send it again, or send what I missed?

Charlie: Concerned and fearful for the country, yes. But I'm also concerned for what illegal immigration means for me and for my kids' future.

Joe: So you feel concerned and fearful not only for the country but for what that means for you personally and for your kids' future. Did I get those feelings correct?

Charlie: That's right.

When all three steps are completed, the speaker thanks the dialogue partner for listening and the listener thanks the partner for sharing, followed by a handshake, high five, or, if comfortable, a brief hug. Then they switch roles. The new speaker begins by expressing an appreciation for the new listener's point of view and then moves into stating their view or experience of the subject matter. The new speaker, however, cannot criticize or negate the reality just stated by the dialogue partner, but rather focuses on their own perspective. To do otherwise would immediately dispel the safety created in the Space-Between.

SC Dialogue Step 3: Empathy

After the speaker confirms the accuracy of the validation statement, dialogue partners can use the following sentence stem to express empathy: "Given what you shared, I imagine you might feel _____ [use emotional terms: hurt, frustrated, disappointed, lonely, relieved, relaxed, and so on]."

1. Then, check on the accuracy of the empathy: "Did I get that?" or "Did I get your feeling?"
2. Invite additional feelings: "Are there other feelings?

It's possible Joe might see things differently. In his view, maybe illegal immigration is a result of the US government's involvement in tearing up countries, that warrants a refugee's need to flee, and that the answer to illegal immigration is to lessen America's military involvement in other countries. And maybe Joe's perception of overinvolvement reminds him of his authoritarian household with an abusive dad.

The point of dialogue is not to convince the other of one's truth; it is to share where one stands, respectfully. The fear of financial insecurity can stand side by side with the fear of authoritarian rule. In the process, Joe and Charlie might come to realize that while they have different views of how to handle the immigration issue, they have common ground. They agree there is a problem or a crisis that needs to be addressed. They might disagree on the "how" but agree on the "what." That is the stepping stone to cocreation and collaboration. And they simultaneously begin to strip away the personal histories that fuel their hostile perceptions.

THE CHALLENGES AND BENEFITS OF EMPATHIZING

Expressing empathy elicits the same internal shift as the rest of the SC Dialogue: a movement through the dialogue toward restoring connection and joyful aliveness. Empathy helps distinguish between the deed and the doer, between what our partner says or does and the person our partner inherently is.

Yet empathy can be challenging. To imagine, much less to experience, when one or both dialogue partners are feeling hurt and angry requires shifting out of one's own experience into the experience of another. Although speakers may have difficulty expressing or confirming feelings, most of the challenges with empathizing revolve around the listener.

For example, the listener may:

- be internally judging the speaker's feelings,
- be reacting to feelings of guilt for having caused the dialogue partner's painful emotions,
- feel uncomfortable expressing strong emotions due to cultural and socialization experiences, or
- be afraid of getting absorbed into the dialogue partner's hurt and misery, especially if they have had similarly painful experiences.

But again, starting with positive messages, gentle guidance, practice, and time, those engaged in an SC Dialogue can overcome these challenges. Additionally, the speaker and listener may need to carefully monitor their breathing and thoughts to feel safe and secure in the conversation and, if necessary, take a temporary pause to re-ground themselves.

The Benefits of SC Dialogue

The goals of an SC Dialogue are both uncommon and profound. Every step—mirroring, validation, and empathy—offers both speaker and listener a golden opportunity for something intangible, something that cannot be bought with money: differentiation and connection.

While common ground can often be discovered in SC Dialogue, it is not the goal of a Dialogue. The goal is to fully understand two perspectives side by side.

When we accept the limited nature of our own perceptions and move into curiosity, a whole world opens up to us, bursting with opportunities. Successful conversations are characterized by safety, curiosity, and respect.

SC Dialogue restores connection if the rules are followed and the technique is practiced. It can be the engine of transformation. Just as no one would expect to be a good skier without diligently exercising the muscles that are required to snowplow, no one can expect a complete change in perception and communication without dutiful practice of the skills of SC Dialogue.

Once learned, SC Dialogue can be used in *all* contexts for many purposes: establishing more pleasant interactions, exchanging information, negotiating tricky compromises, airing grievances, and so on.

The Resistance to SC Dialogue

The two biggest complaints we encounter in teaching SC Dialogue methods are:

1. No one talks this way!
2. It takes so long!

NO ONE TALKS THIS WAY!

Often, people feel our method has a stilted structure. It's likely to strike some people as an unnatural, even stultifying way to converse. And they may rebel against it. And that is okay. It is a strict structure, for a purpose.

To become proficient in accounting, coding, basketball, speaking a new language, or playing the violin requires consistent practice to achieve proficiency. All skills require learning and practicing certain behaviors until they are integrated.

As you practice SC Dialogue, you will become less resistant. With practice, SC Dialogue becomes less artificial and more natural. And it is also true that sometimes mirroring alone may be sufficient for effective communication that is not fraught with emotions. But if you want to move beyond communication to communion, then you need to include all three steps.

IT TAKES SO LONG!

Think of SC Dialogue as the long way that makes your journey shorter. While it may take longer to have conversations using the SC Dialogue process, all your conversations will ultimately become more efficient because small frustrations don't quickly spiral out of control into a period of prolonged, resentful silence.

How to Talk with Anyone about Anything

Yes, it can be awkward and tedious at first. But it is also necessary, humbling, and transformational for anyone trying to overcome differences of opinion and viewpoint with customers, coworkers, friends, family, and out in the world.

CHAPTER 4

Empathy with Everyone

The expression of empathy is the most important connecting skill we humans have. It is our ability to understand and relate to the feelings and perspectives of others. But that capacity seems to be in short supply in these polarized and testy times. Too often, people with opposing views go on the attack rather than try to understand each other and find common ground to work out—or work around—their differences.

This is a problem because, historically, our success as a race—and our happiness and fulfillment as individuals—depends so much on connecting, communicating, interacting, working, and coexisting with one another.

The skill of empathy helps generate safety and connection in all of our relationships and interactions. While our rational skills help us understand what others say, our empathy allows us to discern the feelings and meaning behind the words. This is how we mentally read the spaces of silence that words cannot reach.

The process of empathy begins and ends with curiosity and wonder. It communicates to the listener a respect for their feelings and perspective even if you don't have the same feelings or point of view. Successful leaders—especially those in elected government positions but also in businesses and organizations—have to be able to understand the viewpoints of opponents if they hope to win their cooperation and support through compromise and collaboration.

A 2021 study of 889 employees by Catalyst found that the positive effects of empathy include innovation, engagement, retention, inclusivity, and work-life balance: "We found that empathy is an important driver of employee outcomes such as innovation, engagement, and inclusion—especially in times of crisis. In short, empathy is a must-have in today's workplace."[1]

The employees interviewed in the study were found to be looking for companies where leaders and managers have empathy for the challenges faced by their employees and respond with more flexible and remote-work options and greater racial equity and inclusion "in a world where rapid change is the norm and a technological revolution is fundamentally transforming work."[2]

As a couple, we learned early on that it was a mistake to merely assume we knew what each of us needed from the other. We needed to take the time to be curious, ask questions, listen, and understand what we wanted from each other. The same holds true in all relationships, which is why empathy is so important.

We noted earlier that we created the SC Dialogue process initially as a response to a fight we were having early in our relationship. At that time, we primarily focused on helping couples listen more productively. We realized the importance of empathy in our work with a couple we will call Dawn and Henry, who were caught in their own seemingly intractable impasse.

Dawn's complaint was that Henry always replaced her perspective with his own, and then he added insult to injury by saying she did not make sense. When they came to us, their primary issue of contention was where to send their son to college. Dawn and Henry could not agree on which college they thought their son should attend, and they paid little heed to where the son himself wanted to go.

They'd reached a point where they knew they needed help in making a decision, so they came to us, which was good, but the decision had to be made in two weeks, which didn't give us much time to resolve their long-standing issues in communicating as a couple.

When introduced to the SC Dialogue process, they readily became engaged. In fact, they were among the first couples with whom we experimented with dialogue. Both were intelligent and equally articulate, but they had difficulty listening to the end of a sentence, so they had to be highly regulated by us facilitating a dialogue.

After several tries, Henry, who spoke with authority, managed to mirror Dawn with enough accuracy that she felt heard. She was moved to tears, saying, "That is the first time in my life I have ever felt heard," which astonished Henry.

Then she mirrored Henry as he laid out his authoritative analysis of the positive features of his university of choice. Also after several tries, Dawn finally mirrored him accurately enough that he accepted it, but he was not as emotionally moved by being heard.

For Henry, being heard was not his concern. His concern was being "right." So in the next round, when Dawn validated his perspective by saying, "I can see how you see it that way," he saw her statement as agreeing. We had to do a little more work for him to understand that Dawn "seeing" how Henry felt was different from "agreeing" with how he felt. This helped Henry validate Dawn in the next round, which he did by saying, as Dawn had said, "I get it, and I can see how it looks like that to you." Before we could intervene to redirect him from further responding, though, he said, "But you know that's crazy." Although Dawn flinched, we directed her to mirror him rather than react, since they knew how to do that.

As we progressed with Dawn and Henry from validation to empathy, we had a deep insight. We saw empathy as a sort of acknowledgment that other people had feelings about what they were talking about.

Henry, following our instructions, said to Dawn: "I can imagine that when I don't see things your way and call you crazy, that makes you feel insulted and probably angry, and maybe sad and alone." We coached Henry to look at Dawn in the eyes and ask, "Are those your feelings?" This led Dawn to a very deep emotional response.

As Henry was naming her possible feelings, Dawn's body began to tremble, and she broke down, sobbing. When she regained her composure, Henry had moved closer. He took her hand, and she said, "I don't know what happened. It was like darkness was replaced with light." Then, looking Henry in the eyes, Dawn said, "I felt visible for the first time in my life." Spoiler alert: once they broke their impasse and connected, Henry and Dawn decided to let their son decide where he went to college, which was the right decision.

With that session, we became more interested in using empathy in our therapy process with couples. We engaged in a lot of research and experimentation with other couples, which convinced us to make it a mandatory part of the SC Dialogue process.

It clearly is the most powerful connecting interaction of all the steps of the process. Later, as we moved our work into the public realm with organizations such as schools and corporations, we discovered that when empathic statements are made by bosses to employees, or by employees to their boss or colleagues, the environment becomes refreshingly safe, and productivity goes up.

We have found over many years that empathy is appropriate everywhere and under all circumstances. It is fundamentally human.

Empathy vs. Sympathy

Empathy and *sympathy* are not the same, though they are sometimes confused. There are four subtle but important distinctions between the two terms. The distinctions between these concepts are particularly relevant to our ability to communicate productively and to build and sustain healthy relationships.

1. DIFFERENT IMPACTS

Sympathy involves feelings of pity or sorrow. In sympathy, you share the feelings of others. For example, you feel sad when a friend is sad. But with empathy, you understand the other person's sadness even though you may not feel sad yourself.

Empathy is often expressed as "walking in the shoes" of another person. It is more about understanding and seeking to understand the other person's feelings and perspectives. We suspend our own feeling state to imagine the feeling state of another. But we are only imagining. We never fully know the other. In this way, empathy involves a simultaneous knowing and not knowing.

Expressing sympathy can be tricky, especially outside of close personal relationships, because it is often based on assumptions. For instance, when Caroline learned that a coworker, Cheryl, was demoted from a managerial position to a lower-level job, she asked her to lunch and told her she was sorry about the change.

"Oh, don't say that. I'm very happy," Cheryl said. "In fact, I asked to leave management because my daughter only has one more year of high school before leaving for college and I want to spend more time with her while I can."

In this case, Caroline's sympathetic response was off target, even though it was well-intentioned. If she had been more empathic, Caroline might have asked Cheryl how she felt about the job change before assuming that sympathy was the correct response. Understanding that sympathy and empathy have different impacts leads us to the second important difference between the two.

2. THE ROLE OF COGNITION

In sympathy, we often get caught up in the emotions of others with little thinking (prefrontal cortex processing) on our part. Our sympathetic reactions are often unconscious and unmediated by cognition. Our affect spontaneously fuses into or with the other's affect. We don't plan our sympathetic response. It comes forth on its own when we are in the presence of the other person's intense feelings.

Empathy, however, is an act of volition. In empathy, we choose to try to understand, and we use cognition to regulate our affect. We feel with someone but refuse to fuse with or presume to fully feel the feelings of the other person. Empathy is the experience of both a connection with and a differentiation from the other.

When Caroline offered her sympathetic response to Cheryl, she expressed an immediate, automatic outpouring of feelings of concern and support. She assumed her friend needed soothing. An empathic response, on the other hand, would be more thoughtful. Caroline might have instead first asked questions, such as: "How do you feel about the job change?" "Is there anything I can do to help you make this transition?" "How does your family feel about it?"

The emotion of empathy is as strong as sympathy, but it is framed within a larger perspective that includes factors the other person might not be able to address, such as, *What does this mean for my career long term, or for my retirement plans?*

In sympathy, the self fuses more into the emotional state of the other in order to lend support. In empathy, cognition helps the self retain a differentiated state in order to connect with deeper feeling and greater understanding. It invites a balance of both a separate (cognitive) as well as a connected (emotional) knowing.

While checking with her coworker, Caroline might have discovered that Cheryl was relieved to have less responsibility and the freedom to spend more time with her daughter. Empathy would have helped her discover Cheryl's feelings rather than assume she knew what her coworker was going through.

Caroline could have separated her feelings from Cheryl's. The distinct role of cognition leads to the third main difference between sympathy and empathy, which speaks to the very nature of the sympathetic and empathic relationships.

3. INTERPERSONAL DYNAMIC

The dynamics of sympathy are expressed in a top-down, hierarchal way. The sympathizer takes the active role, and the listener is a passive object. The connotation is that sympathetic feelings, like pity or concern, are "bestowed" onto another.

In contrast, empathy is more horizontal and mutual. The empathizer is simply there beside the other person, respecting the space that holds them both. With gentle questions, the give-and-take in the empathic relationship has a chance to assess more accurately the other person's needs, and, thus, touch them in a meaningful way.

As the empathizer, you slow down, suspend your thoughts, and move into silence in order to learn about the subjective state of the other person. This receptivity to learning new information puts the listener on a profound journey of discovering another person's essence.

It invites them to open their heart to all sorts of new discoveries and learn about the wonder of who the other person actually is. The exchange of affect and information results in a powerful energy flow in both directions. Some who have experienced this energy exchange say that when this happens, the space between the two people feels sacred.

There is a sense that this Space-Between, once respectfully honored, contains the unrealized potential and the mystery that is the ground of all being. The two individuals move toward greater mutual understanding, even if they don't agree on everything, or anything for that matter. This movement past contact and connection into mutual understanding brings us to the fourth distinction between sympathy and empathy.

4. MUTUAL TRANSFORMATION

Because of the hierarchical nature of sympathy, there is little transformation, if any, of either the speaker or the listener. It is a one-way street of assumptions and fusion. In contrast, empathy becomes a revolving door for meaning, integration, and transformation.

There is a gentle push-pull that elicits new information and understanding. The act of speaking and empathizing is a way of "meaning-making" for oneself and for one's partner.

Theologian Nelle Morton referred to this dynamic as

"hearing each other into speech."[3] As recipients of empathic listening, we discover a new vocabulary about our own experiences. The sacred and respectful space between us becomes the breeding ground of information, an ebb and flow of new discoveries within our relationships, and, simultaneously, within the selves.

When you become available to fully listen to others express their emotions, perhaps you will discover things about their lives that help you better understand their viewpoints, which may help you communicate without conflict.

For example, childhood friends Jennifer and Kathy had reconnected online after more than a decade, during which both had married and moved to opposite ends of the country. But their renewed friendship was threatened by the discovery that they had very different political views, primarily because of their opposing views on abortion.

Jennifer was pro-choice. Kathy was pro-life. The topic of abortion had never come up when they were children, so the two women were at first taken aback when they realized their views were so different. Fortunately, they were both empathic women who made the effort to understand each other's positions and the experiences and feelings behind them.

In the dynamic process of listening and sharing, layers were peeled away, and they began to discover things they had not known about each other, which included experiences they'd had since childhood.

Empathy invites an inner excavation of hidden thoughts and feelings that makes it safe to bring them to the surface. It allows the speaker to formulate, express, and share ideas and feelings that may not have been realized or expressed ever before. Both speaker and listener become enlarged and transformed by the stillness of listening in this way.

Looking at these differences, we can see that sympathy is often our first and most primitive reaction to someone else's dilemma. Empathy, which requires greater consciousness and often intentional practice, is a more highly evolved response, requiring more prefrontal cortex functioning. It's not surprising, then, that empathy is a more recent concept in our understanding of relationship. Over the centuries, our instinct to sympathize gained the addition of higher cerebral processing, and the concept of empathy was born.

Empathy and Safe Conversations Dialogue

With SC Dialogue, we meet one of our greatest challenges: accepting the otherness of those we interact with. Without accepting otherness, we fail to make true connection. Empathy helps us learn about a consciousness that is not our own. We are invited to accept that others are different from us and, thus, may have different worldviews.

Our task, then, is to visit their worlds and imagine how they might feel, as well as what experiences and mindsets are behind those feelings. Empathy allows us to discover the otherness of people who come into our lives and to reflect on it, discerning its meaning and integrating this new understanding into our consciousness.

In the experience of giving and receiving empathy, we discover things in the lives of others that help us feel what they are feeling. Within the give-and-take of empathy, we experience vulnerability when we open ourselves to hearing with curiosity and speaking without self-editing. SC Dialogue allows us to practice using vulnerability as a strength as we learn more about each other.

There is an ever-widening circle here. Mutual empathy allows both parties to feel safe enough to become vulnerable. When empathizing, we allow others to appear without judgment or categorization, even after we have developed some understanding of their experience. When the spirit of safety is created, we can each cautiously emerge from behind our walls, give language to unarticulated thoughts and feelings, and reveal more of our authentic selves to one another.

Empathy can help us truly hear each other, because when there is receptivity and a safe space, words will flow. The listener is like a beacon in the fog, a signpost of solidity that allows the speaker to journey forth into often strange and scary lands. Empathy invites us to question and excavate hidden stories that will continue sabotaging our relationships unless they are told and understood in a conscious light.

Lastly, empathy plays an essential role in facilitating growth and healing. When we allow ourselves to be vulnerable, we open the door to mutually respond to our wounds with empathy. Through this connected emotional experiencing, we are inspired into action.

Empathy ultimately motivates speakers to stretch beyond their comfort zone in the service of the other. It requires a great deal of courage, as the listeners open themselves to truly receive. The experience of reciprocity can narrow the space between individuals with differences and heal the wounds that have separated them.

Just as a cut on the skin is slowly knit back together by the incremental joining and growth of new skin, the experience of empathic connection and dialogue can also serve to heal what had been severed. In empathy, we invite, we discover, we listen, we heal, and we become whole.

When we listen with empathy, we attend from a place of emotional intelligence and connection rather than from a distant, judgmental stance. When empathy is flowing in both directions, we see beyond the other person's emotions. We then begin to move into a sense of understanding and away from conflict.

The New Consciousness of Empathy

The word *empathy* emerged in the last one hundred years and became identified as one of the central processes within psychotherapy. This suggests that the spread of the concept also might be signaling a developing consciousness within our nature as a human species.

As the world we live in moves toward a global dialogue, empathy is playing a central role in the development of a new consciousness. At the core of this new sense is our capacity for feeling ourselves into the hearts and minds of others, for listening and understanding without judgment, and for learning the art of true communion.

Empathy is an innately and uniquely human response. It's time that we realize what a powerful force our capacity for empathy truly is. It invites a Copernican shift away from revolving around ourselves toward an expanded orbit that includes both ourselves *and* the others who inhabit our universe.

Whenever we speak, listen, and relate to another person without judgment, we are transforming the world one person at a time. We are manifesting our connectedness and creating a world that is safer than the one we now inhabit. We already have this power for transformation. Let's act on it for the sake of ourselves and the world we share.

CHAPTER 5

Practice Zero Negativity

As you know by now, the roots of SC Dialogue sprouted in the early struggles in our own marriage and were grown to maturity in our work with couples. The concept of Zero Negativity was created about twenty years later, when we were on the verge of divorce. Lawyers had been hired, but neither of us had made a final decision.

While waiting for our feelings to crystallize, we decided to take a weekly break from our marital warfare and go on a date. To prevent possible conflict, we decided to do something we both enjoyed so we would not have to make any decisions.

We love libraries and bookstores, so we hit the books—in particular one large bookstore in New York City. Given the tempestuous state of our marriage, we normally spent most of our bookstore time searching for solutions in the Marriage, Psychology, or Therapy sections, but on this date day we veered into the Astrology section.

This was not familiar territory for either of us, so we thought it might be a safe haven. Perusing the shelves, we spied a very large book on astrology for couples. Intrigued, we pulled it off the shelf, sat on the floor, and started flipping through the pages looking for our astrological signs.

Since neither of us believed in such esoteric literature, it was sort of fun but not serious—until we spied a section that described the relationship between our two matched astrological signs: Virgo and Aquarius. *This should be interesting*, we thought, laughing at the silly idea that our lives and our relationship could somehow be determined by the alignment of the stars.

The essay began with a description of our personalities—as prescribed by our astrological signs—and it was mostly on the mark. Our curiosity got the best of us. We read on to the section about what sort of relationship Virgos and Aquarians could expect to have.

Our mockery of the book turned into a shock of recognition. The description hit home. The specific paragraph that changed our lives was not very long. As we recall, it said Virgo and Aquarius couples have very intense relationships, especially negatively. They tend to observe each other with continuous and ruthless scrutiny.

We looked at each other with wide eyes. Had someone been spying on us? While we were not accustomed to seeking information from astrology, this sentence seemed quite accurate.

We fled the bookstore and went to lunch. We needed to process this information. We spent the meal discussing this unexpected revelation from an unscientific source. In the course of our conversation, we made several decisions.

First, Helen proposed that we get a calendar from the bookstore, keep a record of any negative exchange on each day, and mark those days with a black X. If we got through a day without a negative exchange, we would give ourselves a red check mark.

Second, we decided to give ourselves nine months to monitor our negativity, then decide the future of our marriage. During the first month, we earned a black X every day. We did a little better in the second month, earning a few red checks on those days when we kept it positive. It was not until the third month that we went a full week without any black marks for being negative. Later we finally achieved a month without a black X.

The trend continued to be positive, and at the end of nine months we had had three consecutive months with only positive scores. There was hope! And so, instead of filing for divorce, we decided to recommit to our marriage and planned a small but full recommitment service on New Year's Eve and threw a party with 250 guests. Since our recommitment party was in a room with views overlooking the Hudson River, where the New Year's Eve fireworks would occur, we decided to claim the city's celebration as our own.

We'd had our share of marital fireworks, after all, so why not embrace them and enjoy the way they brought dazzling light to the darkness? Our commitment to Zero Negativity was sealed that night, which is why we remain happily married to this day.

At first, we thought this might be just a personal exercise for us and not appropriate to introduce to other couples. However, because of its transformative impact on us, its relevance to all couples became apparent. We had discovered that any thriving relationship has to have one nonnegotiable quality: safety. And it is obvious that safety and negativity are incompatible.

Given the logic of that awareness, we made Zero Negativity an integral part of our work with couples, and eventually we made it a part of our core theory, which was taught and demonstrated to every therapist in our training programs globally. We now give it the status "nonnegotiable" if you want a great relationship.

We see Zero Negativity (ZN) as the third skill in SC Dialogues. ZN essentially involves eliminating put-downs, name-calling, eye rolls, or any other form of shame, blame, or criticism of anyone with whom you communicate each day. That's what we decided to do for each other, and we recommend it to everyone, everywhere—at work, at worship, at play, in the classroom, the halls of Congress—all human ecosystems.

This may seem like an *obvious* thing to do. How can you communicate productively and build solid relationships by insulting and disparaging your coworkers, supervisors, clients, partners, or others with whom you interact on a daily basis?

Negativity is a major source of stress in all those relationships. Consistent research has associated negativity with anger and depression, which in turn are associated with suppressing our immune systems, making us vulnerable to disease and, thus, interfering with our health and shortening our life spans by as much as thirteen years.[1] Negativity is clearly a dysfunctional interaction that seems endemic in the human race, a chronic pandemic more destructive than any virus that has threatened us.

But you don't have to spend much time scrolling through social media posts or listening to conversations on podcasts and talk radio—or even in work meetings and dinner parties—before the rebukes and insults start flying between those who have differing opinions and perspectives.

It can get ugly, and all too often it does. Liberals attack conservatives by calling them racists and elitists. Conservatives disparage liberals as "lib-tards." Anti-abortion advocates assail pro-abortion opponents as "baby killers." Pro-choice advocates attack pro-life opponents as misogynists and religious zealots. Even terms once considered positive, such as *woke* and *politically correct*, have been co-opted, weaponized, and hurled as insults in today's brutally polarized political environment.

Nothing productive comes of these tactics. Negativity only stirs anxiety, inflaming debates and discussions into angry confrontations. We know this, yet it is all too easy to give in to our worst impulses by going on the attack when we feel threatened. If your boss criticizes you for being unproductive, it is tempting to fire back, "You just expect me to do all the work so you can take all the credit."

We understand that eliminating negativity in your interactions is not easy, but it is also a goal worthy of pursuing if you really want to build bridges and find common ground in your workplace, your community, your organizations, and your circle of acquaintances. Why does negativity seem to be everywhere, and why does eliminating it seem so hard?

These are really great questions, and there is a really good answer from brain science research. Getting a handle on this may help us understand ourselves and others when we fall into that negative space.

Thousands of years ago, all humans lived in environments in which there was no security like we have now. No social rules and no one regulating how we interacted with one another, like a police force. We all lived in hostile environments, and danger was everywhere, from wild animals to human beings from other tribes.

Our brains evolved in this dangerous environment and developed a "negativity bias." Since the main purpose of the brain is to survive, we could not afford to assume that an animal we saw on the path or a person who was approaching us was friendly.[2]

If you made a wrong decision back then, you became prey. So the safest response was to assume the worst until there were no signs of danger. Then we would approach and eat or hunt or play together.

Although we now have security systems—police, sheriffs, military—that default negativity bias is still in place, and we have to manage it all the time. So your problem with negativity is not your fault. It is just your brain trying to protect you.

Knowing all this does not excuse any of us for not looking for a better way. The best protection now is to use the SC Dialogue process to talk about your differences and collaborate on win-win solutions.

Take the Pledge

Negativity is toxic energy that destroys safety and, thus, prevents connecting in relationships. Removing negativity from all your relationships is so important that we recommend embracing this concept by taking a Zero Negativity Pledge, which encourages you to focus on treating others around you with a positive, hopeful, and gracious attitude.

When you remove the negative energy and attitude from your conversations, you will be able to deal more efficiently with difficult or challenging issues because a negative charge does not overload them.

Here is an example of a Zero Negativity Pledge:

I pledge to make all of my relationships and conversations zones of Zero Negativity for the next thirty days by omitting from all my interactions any words, tones, or body language that could be experienced as a put-down and are not productive or healing.

If I experience a negative reaction from someone and feel threatened, I will immediately send a gentle signal to communicate that I have experienced a put-down and then use the Reconnecting Process to restore safety and to connect.

Signed _____

Date _____

Countering Negativity with the Zero Negativity Reconnecting Process

What do you do if you are the target of negativity in a conversation with a coworker, supervisor, or anyone you often deal with? When someone puts you down or slights you, it is natural to feel hurt, stressed, and threatened. So it's important to repair any fissure or disconnection if you want to keep the conversation productive and the relationship intact.

Here are some guidelines for dealing with negativity when you feel targeted.

SAY SOMETHING

Don't assume that those who say negative things to you know you're upset. Some people are so consistently negative that they are not even aware of it. Thus, they might not be able to see that their words were hurtful. They simply assume they are being normal, and you are just too sensitive.

Some people lack empathy or the ability to read the reactions of those they offend. So let the negative person know that they've crossed your boundary with their negative comments. You can do this without going on the counterattack and escalating the war of words.

We advise against accusing them of projecting their own traits onto you. That tends not to work. We recommend trying gentle signals in first-person language, such as, "Ouch, I felt that zinger!" Or, "I experience that as a little harsh." Or, "I don't think I deserve that. I would like to keep this positive, shall we?"

This signal is important for the safety of the two engaged in dialogue. You want to acknowledge if you're hurt and if something doesn't land right. And you want the other person to know that the words were hurtful so that the conversation doesn't continue to be negative.

In any relationship or interaction, there are bound to be moments in which negativity slips in, intentionally or otherwise. Remember the negativity bias. None of us are perfectly attuned and sensitive to the needs of everyone around us. Our brain operates on its own to obey its prime directive: to keep us safe and alive. So we have to work hard to build healthy relationships that allow us to reconcile when we have differences, heal, and move forward in a more positive direction.

Your response to being attacked is wired into your brain and operates independent of your will, so when you feel threatened, you have to be very thoughtful about how you create safety. When you understand this and become conscious of it, you are better able to respond in a positive manner and steer the conversation on a more productive track.

FOLLOW A RECONNECTING PROCESS THAT WORKS FOR YOU

When a negative interaction has occurred:

1. Ask for a do-over. Tell your conversation partner, "This negativity isn't working for either of us. Let's try this

again." Take a time-out from the conversation for a little mental-health break, start over, and try reframing the conversation in a more positive manner.

2. Mirror and suggest language that is more positive and not hurtful. "If you aren't happy with my performance, please suggest some ways that I can be more productive rather than criticizing me." Or, "I know we disagree on this topic, but let's try to understand each other and keep it positive rather than attacking each other."

3. Offer a way to reconnect. "Why don't we take a break, have a cup of coffee somewhere, and find a way to resolve our differences and move forward?"

4. Have a Safe Conversation about the feelings that came up. "When I heard I wasn't invited, I felt hurt. Did I do something to upset you?"

5. Offer a gift or change in behavior. That might include a sincere apology from each of you; offering each other three appreciations: a kind note, an exchange of gifts, having a meal together; or any combination of these.

Turn Frustrations into Requests

Another means of dealing with negativity when you feel targeted involves our Frustrations Dialogue, which we think is so important that we are devoting the rest of this chapter to discuss it in detail.

We've found that you can help create and maintain Zero Negativity in your interactions by managing your frustrations and turning them into requests. You can do this on your own as well as develop a process to do it with family members, bosses, coworkers, and anyone else you deal with on a regular basis.

Here's a quick example of managing your frustrations to avoid negativity on your own:

Linda was a very orderly housekeeper. Her teenage daughter Julie was not.

As a result, they butted heads. Linda found herself saying negative things like, "You are such a mess! How can you live like this?"

You can imagine how her teenager responded. Let's just say Julie didn't transform overnight into Tidy Teen.

Linda realized she needed to find a new approach to avoid warfare on the home front. So she managed her frustration by asking Julie to join her at their favorite pizza parlor for a mother-daughter dinner one night. There, over Julie's favorite pineapple pizza, Linda apologized for saying negative things about her and the state of her bedroom.

"You know me. I like to keep the house neat and clean. It helps me feel in control and secure, so I get frustrated when that doesn't seem as important to you. But I don't want to fight with you over that anymore. Do you have any suggestions on how to ease my frustration and keep our relationship positive?"

"Yes, I do, Mom," Julie said.

"What do you suggest?" Linda asked.

"Don't go into my room!" Julie said. "That way you won't see how messy it is, and you won't get frustrated."

Using the SC Dialogue process, Linda mirrored: "You're saying that I should not go into your room, then I won't see the mess. Am I getting that?"

"You got it, Mom."

"Thanks for that suggestion, but I'm not sure that's an option I can live with," Linda said. "I will still know that there's a mess in there, even if I don't look."

"I understand that, Mom, but here's the key to reframing this situation. I graduate from high school in six months. Then, a few months later, I will go off to college. When I'm gone, you can clean my room every day if you want. I won't be there to mess it up anymore. I know you will miss me—if not my messy ways. And I will miss you—if not your relentless tidiness. So for now, let's just enjoy having each other around. What do you say?"

A truce was reached. Negativity was banished. Linda stayed out of Julie's room, knowing that within a few months, she might even miss her daughter and the chaos of her room.

This is a simple example of two people working toward Zero Negativity through Safe Conversations, collaboration, and cooperation. Instead of arguing and attacking each other, they found a way to stay on a more positive track. Linda and Julie did this in an informal, conversational way, but we also have developed a more structured dialogue for those involved in more complicated situations.

Our Frustrations Dialogue provides a step-by-step process for stating your frustrations and making requests to keep your interactions safe and positive. It offers a series of sentence stems that follows three simple steps:

1. Ask for a meeting to share a frustration: "Is now a good time to share a frustration I have?"
2. State the frustration briefly as a behavior you want changed: "I get frustrated when I turn in a report and do not get any feedback for several weeks."
3. Suggest ways this frustration can be turned into an opportunity for a more positive change: "What I would like is, if you cannot give feedback immediately after I turn in a report, for you to acknowledge by email that you received the report and give me a date when you will respond."

We know that even a structured dialogue can break down when two or more people involved in a conversation become contentious over differing views and agendas. The fact is that most people do not know what they want. They know they have a negative feeling yet desire a positive one, but they have difficulty describing a behavior that would evoke that positive feeling. And they are more likely to let you know only what they *do not* want because their primary focus is to stop their discomfort.

It's easier to point at problems and play the blame game than it is to take responsibility for collaborating to find creative solutions. And that makes sense. But without clarity on a specific behavior that would change their feelings, little progress toward their goal of removing their discomfort can be achieved.

Creating safety and a sense of "we are all in this together, despite our differences" provides that safe space for seeking solutions.

Turn Frustrations into a Wish for Change

To reiterate and elaborate, the Frustration Dialogue begins with you asking for a meeting, whether formal or informal: "When is a good time for me to share a frustration I'm experiencing?" It's important that a specific time is set and kept by both parties. Predictability helps create safety.

At the meeting, you share your frustration as an objective experience, not as a criticism. If you criticize the other person, the focus of the conversation will likely be on a defense against the criticism rather than on the frustration.

An example of a criticism-free frustration statement might be:

"As your supervisor, I become frustrated when you don't respond promptly to my emails." This is just reporting a fact; it does not contain any reference to the person's character.

Or from the opposing point of view: "You are my boss. I understand that. But I get frustrated when you send me emails with questions or requests that require me to put aside what I'm working on so I can respond to them. Then, when I don't get my work done on schedule, you give me a bad job review."

Following the SC Dialogue design, the other person then mirrors what you have said, noting that they have listened and understand the source of your frustration. In this way, a sense of safety is established and a connection is made, giving both sides a foundation from which to work.

Next, you suggest ways that the other person can alleviate your frustrations by offering solutions, shifting from a negative to a positive track, and moving from conflict to connection. In addition, you move from the abstract of a feeling to a concrete behavior. If your request is abstract or vague—*I want to feel valued*—the other person will fill in the blank with something concrete from their inner world, and what they do will most likely not be what you want.

An example of a concrete solution would be to say, "My only request is that you immediately acknowledge when you have received my emails. You don't have to stop what you're doing and find answers to my questions or resolve the issues in the email; just let me know that it's on your to-do list."

Or you might say to your boss, "Rather than interrupting my flow to answer your questions, can I simply acknowledge that I've received your message and then go on with what I was doing, as long as I get back to you with a response within twenty-four hours? Would that work?"

Make sure your requests are always positive and specific. Do not request that the other person *stop*, *quit*, or *refrain from* doing something. Omit all absolutes, such as *always* and *never*.

Your requests should follow the SMART plan and be Specific, Measurable, Attainable, Relevant, and Time-bound.

Alternative Zero Negativity Methods for Turning Frustrations into Requests

We get it. Often, you don't have the time or need for a formal Frustrations Dialogue. In these cases, you can simply use the Safe Conversations ideas to change the energy of your interactions.

AT WORK

Let's say you have a coworker who ignores you or seems to avoid you. Instead of feeling put off and showing your frustration by saying something negative, such as, "Why do you treat me like a potted plant?" you might want to stay positive and make a request or offer a friendly invitation, such as:

- "I've noticed you're really good at your job. Would you mind giving me some tips so I can find ways to get better at mine?"
- "You seem to work efficiently and meet all your deadlines. I could use any guidance you might have on how to do that."
- "You handle our boss's demands so much better than I do. Can you tell me how you do that?"

SOCIALLY

Maybe you are frustrated with your cousin because she is often late, or your bachelor friend wants to meet at a bar that frequently leads to all-night drinking, or your sister visits your home with her two dogs that make themselves comfortable on your living room furniture. You might want to say something like:

- "If we agree to meet at a restaurant and you're running late, would you mind calling or texting me to let me know?"
- "I'm not sure meeting at a bar after work and drinking for a couple of hours is the healthiest thing for me. How about meeting at the gym and working out together instead?"
- "I love both of your Irish Wolfhounds, but if you want to bring them out with us, maybe we should plan on eating somewhere with outdoor seating rather than in my apartment."

Remember, learning to ask specifically for what you want can transform your relationships from negative to positive, and it empowers the other person to be effective in their response to your wishes. If you channel your frustrations into requests with grace and strength, the chances for success are better.

To do that, we suggest you:

1. Speak with a kind tone of voice. Make sure your posture and bearing are friendly.
2. Look the other person in the eyes, with soft eyes, and let them know you want to stay positive.
3. Speak succinctly. No rambling. No mansplaining—or womansplaining.
4. Make an actionable request. Because this is so important,

saying, "I want to feel respected" is not an actionable request, even if it is your goal. Give the other person something more specific. Doing so will help achieve the same goal but provide an actionable path for the other person: "I would like the opportunity to attend your morning meetings with the rest of our team."

5. Remember, you can always use the Frustrations Dialogue if more informal conversations fail to attain Zero Negativity.

COUNTER NEGATIVITY WITH LAUGHTER

Finally, as our story at the beginning of this chapter illustrates, we have found over the years that one of the greatest ways to overcome negativity and create safety in a relationship is to apply generous doses of humor and irreverence. Laughter truly is the best medicine in many situations.

Life will be more fun, and healthier.

CHAPTER 6

The Practice of Affirmations

Wayne is a researcher who often works with authors as they write their books. One day, he received a telephone call from a bestselling author who was looking for help on a new book.

"Wayne, I've heard so much about you from my editors at my publishing house. They tell me you're probably the best researcher in the field," the author said. "I would like to meet with you to discuss working together on my next book. Would you be willing to fly to Fiji, where I'm staying at a friend's place for the next few months? I won't keep you long. We can meet for a couple of hours and then you can fly home. I mean, I really appreciate your time and talents, so I promise we will make the most of this meeting."

Wayne, who lived in Florida, did a quick calculation: it would take him about twenty hours each way to fly to Fiji and back, and a round-trip ticket would cost about $4,000. All this for a two-hour meeting? And the bestselling author, a man of considerable wealth, had made no mention of compensating him or paying his expenses for this introductory meeting.

"You know, I really appreciate that you thought of me, and I'd be honored to work with you," he told the author. "Would you be willing to pay my travel expenses and compensate me for my time if I agree to come to Fiji and meet with you?"

There was a long silence from the author. Finally, he said, "Well, I appreciate your taking the time to talk with me. I guess this won't work out. Goodbye."

Well, so much for valuing my time and talents, Wayne thought.

Have you ever had the experience of feeling used and abused because it seemed as though someone valued you only when you did what they wanted you to do? Did you feel as though the person manipulated you to serve their purpose but otherwise ignored you?

I'm just a pawn in her game.

He's just using me to do his work for him.

This internal monologue is very common. No one likes to feel used. Yet, there are controlling and manipulative individuals who view every interaction as a transaction. Their attitude says, "What's in it for me?"

It's much more rare to find someone who values and appreciates you even though there is nothing to be gained from your interactions. Are there relationships beyond reciprocity, void of expectation, and, thus, without conditions? We believe there are.

When we developed the Zero Negativity process as the third skill in SC Dialogue, we thought we had all the relational tools anyone would need to restore and maintain connection. After all, what more could people need for connecting despite their differences? We had a structured dialogue, empathy, and Zero Negativity all in place.

But as we interviewed clients about how the SC Dialogue

process was working for them, we learned that it was not enough to be compassionate and avoid negativity. Many felt it was important to add a skill that put the conversation and relationships on a positive track. But our sources did not mean just "being positive" as an attitude. They wanted it to be openly and actively expressed.

Our clients wanted a skill that could be applied to make the person with a differing view feel genuinely valued and affirmed, and, thus, safe to interact with. They wanted to let the other person, or other people, know that they were respected and appreciated in a transformational, not transactional, way.

The idea was to let those we disagree with on some points know that they didn't have to agree with us to be valued. Parents talk about loving their children unconditionally; what we are talking about is a "lite" version of unconditional love. Think of it as "unconditional value and appreciation."

With that in mind, we decided to add affirmation as a fourth skill of SC Dialogue. This turned out to be essential, and it completed the steps that help to create, restore, and sustain connection even with those of differing views and opinions. The magic of the Safe Conversations process is that you feel safe; therefore, you can talk and listen with mutual respect. We see it as an efficient communication tool for the exchange of energy and information, and one where all participants are seen, heard, and valued.

With this structure, safety happens; when safety happens, connecting happens. And connecting ignites a collaborative process that can transform the negative energy of conflict into the vibrant energy of feeling fulfilled, fully engaged in life, and joyful.

The entire SC Dialogue is essentially an affirmation process. The act of listening and mirroring ("Let me see if I got that"), expressing curiosity ("Is there more about that?"), providing validation ("Your view make sense"), and communicating empathy ("I can imagine how you might be feeling")—all of these acts are also affirmation.

We believe affirmation benefits both the giver and the listener. When you put an affirmation out there—"You're really on top of your game today!"—you are engaging part of your brain to put that affirmation into language. When that happens, you experience the affirmation as if it was directed at yourself. Affirmations, then, are a boomerang gift. When you send it off to others, it comes back to regift you. You might think of it as the gift that keeps on giving!

Getting Down to Semantics

Affirmation is both a noun and a verb. It is a stance taken toward another, or others, and also a verbal statement or other behavior that operationalizes the stance. As a noun, *affirmation* is the recognition of the intrinsic value of another person because they exist, not because they have done something for you. It is something that's declared to be true about another person—a positive statement or judgment that is intended to provide encouragement, emotional support, or motivation.

As a verb, *affirmation* is a behavior, a skill that is practiced by asserting affirming words to another person, which creates a state of being affirmed. The words can be simple:

"You are wonderful."

"You have a big heart."

"Your viewpoint is always interesting."

"You have such a unique perspective."

Affirmations are not appreciations. An *appreciation* is a positive response to what someone has done. An *affirmation* is acknowledging that someone is worthy of recognition and valued, not because of what they have done but because they exist. Affirmation is not based on feelings or actions. It is the acknowledgment of someone's intrinsic value.

Affirmation is unconditional acceptance of the other and the celebration of difference. Differentiation requires showing curiosity and acceptance of otherness, showing empathy for the experience of another, and expressing gratitude for the being of the other.

The Steps of Affirmation

Following are the steps of affirmation. Each step deepens the level of affirmation.

I acknowledge that you exist, are different from me, and are not my view of you.

I accept that you exist and that you are different from me.

I appreciate you that you exist and that you are different.

I admire your existence and the difference that you are.

I affirm your existence as valuable beyond any value you are to me.

I advocate for your existence and your difference.

I adore you as you are, your essence, and the difference from me that you are.

As you can see, affirmations have no expectations; thus, there is no disappointment. No transaction or reciprocity takes place;

therefore, there are no regrets or negative memories. When you offer affirmations to someone, they are based on how those individuals experience themselves, not on your expectations based on your needs.

To fully affirm another person, there must be some sacrifices. Affirmation requires you to give up the victim role, which shames others with statements like, "How could you do that to me?" Affirmation also requires the sacrifice of the persecutor role, which disempowers others: "Never mind, I'll do it." Or it devalues someone: "You never get it right." Or it conveys contempt: "You are disgusting."

To affirm others, you must say goodbye to manipulative mind games that use phrases like, "Look at all I have done for you," or "I can never count on you." When you affirm someone, you shift from wanting to giving, from complaining to gratitude, from emptiness to fullness, from the past to the future. You show patience, kindness, confidence, humility, curiosity; you listen without judgment and talk without criticizing.

When you affirm another person at work, in an organization, during a meeting, or in a Zoom call, you accept and advocate for them despite your differences. You acknowledge what they've done well. You convert your frustrations into requests and create positive interactions that make for positive memories. When you affirm others, you remove impatience, unkindness, jealousy, boasting, comparison, arrogance, rudeness, and irritability.

Affirmation Greases the Wheels

Ed is a tech consultant in the health-care industry who often has to deal with medical professionals, including surgeons and other high-powered and successful doctors who aren't always open to technological change. Often, they resist his efforts to introduce them to new telehealth technologies like web-based medical examinations and remote patient monitoring. They might say they are too busy to go to training to learn about new tech, even though it's been shown to improve their workflow and patient satisfaction. In fact, Ed sometimes has to enlist other doctors who serve as "physician champions" to win over doctors who are more receptive when a peer approaches them.

"I've learned to be very tactful in dealing with these highly intelligent, independent-minded, and strong-willed clients," Ed said. "You can't push too hard when they resist change, nor can you be critical of them in any way. I've found the best way to win them over to trying new technologies is to affirm them every step of the way. I tell them that they have successful careers by staying on top of medical science, and these new technologies will help them keep growing and enjoying success well into the future."

As Ed's example illustrates, using words of affirmation can improve your ability to manage negative interactions more efficiently. Avoid using negative words, criticism, or defensive approaches to keep your interactions free of conflict. Be encouraging and affirming to keep it positive and easier to accept.

But using words of affirmation doesn't only improve your relationships or make those you interact with feel good. The implicit gratitude in affirmation has been scientifically proven to make you happier and healthier.[1] Words of affirmation are, after all, expressions of gratitude to those with whom you communicate, acknowledging all that they are and do.

The more you use affirmation language, the more you will find yourself enjoying positive experiences with others. The best thing you can do for yourself is to affirm another person without conditions. Let's take a look at an example from research:

> Managers who remember to say "thank you" to people who work for them may find that those employees feel motivated to work harder. Researchers at the Wharton School at the University of Pennsylvania randomly divided university fund-raisers into two groups. One group made phone calls to solicit alumni donations in the same way they always had. The second group—assigned to work on a different day—received a pep talk from the director of annual giving, who told the fundraisers she was grateful for their efforts. During the following week, the university employees who heard her message of gratitude made 50% more fundraising calls than those who did not.[2]

The Power of Your Influence

We've often heard it said that we should never underestimate the power of our own influence. Whether you're a formal leader or not, people will never forget the impact of being lifted up by your affirming words. Sincere words of affirmation are effortless and have a disproportionate effect on people's self-esteem. Most of us can recall, often word for word, when someone of influence paid us a compliment, whether it was last month or many years ago.

Helen and Harville Share Personal Stories of Affirmation

Please allow us to share some stories of how we have been affected by words of affirmation.

HELEN:

My parents had four children. The oldest was Ray. Next came my older sister, June, then me, and finally, Swanee, the youngest. My sisters, June and Swanee, have always been extroverts who were clear on what they wanted or needed. I have been more of an introvert and more reticent about expressing myself. Instead, I kept my feelings to myself.

When my brother, Ray, and I were both adults, he told me that he had noticed early on that my sisters commanded more attention than I did, and that he always kept an eye on me, checking on me regularly. My parents were very busy people. They hired a nanny to provide daily care for us after Swanee was born; otherwise, we did not get a lot of adult attention.

As the oldest child, Ray took it upon himself to serve as my guardian. Many years into adulthood, he gave me an example of this. Ray said that during our childhood Halloween trips going door-to-door for candy in our neighborhood, he would make sure that my more extroverted sisters didn't claim all the candy. Our big brother made sure I got my share.

Now, that may seem like a small thing, but it meant the world to me because I often felt overshadowed by my more outspoken sisters. They are wonderful people, without a doubt, and widely recognized as accomplished women. Ray's stories about watching out for me, though, have always made me feel that I, too, was valued, worthy, and wonderful in my own ways.

HARVILLE:

I recall two powerful and life-changing affirmations in my life. The first was when I was young and living with my sister on a farm. My parents died before I was six years old and left behind nine children, three of whom ranged from ages six to thirteen and needed guardians. The other six were adults, employed and married. Our father's brother, who lived nearby, championed the idea of sending the three youngest of us to an orphanage. My older sisters rejected that idea. Instead, they divided us up among themselves and took us into their homes.

I was the youngest, and my youngest sister and her husband took me to live with them, although they were quite poor. She was only eighteen and had just married, and she and her husband lived on a subsistence farm in southern Georgia. As she packed me up to go home with her, I recall her saying to our other siblings and to that uncle who wanted us to be sent to an orphanage that "under no circumstances will Harville be sent to an orphanage, ever."

When I was thirteen and ready to go to high school, another one of my sisters, who lived in a small town called Statesboro about a dozen miles from the farm, invited me to come live with her so I could go to a better school near her home. She explained to the sister I was living with: "Harville is a good boy and smart, and I want to be sure he doesn't wind up like the rest of us, having to work for someone else and being poor and uneducated."

That affirmation from my sister, who believed in me and my potential in this world, put me on the road to a classical education that led eventually to doctoral studies at the University of Chicago's Divinity School, which resulted in my becoming a university professor, therapist, and author.

Years after that memorable affirmation from a family member, I received another powerful boost from yet another kind woman. This occurred after our book for couples, *Getting the Love You Want*, was released. Our publisher's marketing team had sent the book out to many media outlets, and one copy went to the executive producer of *The Oprah Winfrey Show*.

We would later learn that the executive producer was in a

troubled relationship, and she was not in the mood to produce a show on a book offering advice to couples. However, her boyfriend read our book and recommended that she share it with Oprah. The famed talk-show host read it, loved it, and invited me on her hit show. In fact, she eventually built seventeen show segments around our couples therapy program over the next twenty years.

There was one particular moment of affirmation from Oprah that I will never forget. After filming one of our couple's workshops for two segments to be shown on two consecutive days of her show, Oprah stepped in front of the camera with the book in hand, pointed to it, and told her television audience something like, "This is the best book on relationships that has ever been written. You sit down right now and write the title down and get yourself to your nearest bookstore, buy it, and read it."

The rest is history. The book made the *New York Times* bestseller list eleven times. In its third edition, thirty years later, it has sold over four million copies and is still going strong. Oprah's words to her audience were both an appreciation and an affirmation. She deeply appreciated the book for the impact it had on her own relationship, then went beyond the personal to offer an even greater affirmation to our work as authors.

Think about this: We gave you four examples of affirmations that meant so much to us or our family over the years. Three of them were from caring family members whose words were spoken only to us. The fourth was from a powerful celebrity with a global reach.

Whether you are someone with the tremendous influence of Oprah or just a loving sibling, friend, coworker, or acquaintance, your words matter in ways that you cannot imagine. Watch for any and all opportunities to affirm the value of those around you, whether they are your team members, siblings, children, neighbors, or strangers. Perhaps most importantly, don't forget to affirm yourself. We often forget to be as kind to ourselves as we strive to be with others.

Affirmations in Actions

Finally, remember that you can demonstrate affirmations, kindness, love, and grace not just through your words but also through your actions, which may be even more powerful and more memorable than your words. Affirmative, caring behaviors are one way you can create safety and positive energy in your relationships. Caring behaviors are an opportunity to let another person know you value them. For example, you might begin by thinking about what you can do to make a person at work feel noticed and appreciated. Maybe it's just bringing them a cup of coffee one day. Or pitching in on a big project. Or taking them to lunch.

Another method of putting affirmations into action is to surprise a person with a random act that shows how much they are valued. Some people don't like being surprised, so you have to be somewhat careful with this, and don't go over the top. You don't need to hire Taylor Swift to sing them a song. We have two rules for using this type of affirmation in action.

1. The surprise must be something that delights the other person—not just you.
2. The surprise should be random and unexpected.

Maybe it's gifting tickets to a Taylor Swift concert. Or offering a gift card to the person's favorite restaurant or clothing store. Maybe it's something as simple as placing a picture frame on a coworker's desk as a surprise.

As we learned in our exploration of the astrology book for couples at the bookstore, sharing a fun experience with someone is another way to break down barriers and take the tension out of communications and relationships. This might involve watching a funny movie together, listening to a comedian on a podcast during a road trip, or adjourning a business meeting for a trip to a museum or zoo. The idea is to engage in something safe and enjoyable to break down walls and create bonds.

Many people have been conditioned to think work is too serious and too important to include moments of enjoyment or fun. So it may take some convincing to get a coworker, family member, or client to relax. In truth, enjoying the company of others is crucial to our feelings of safety and satisfaction, along with making money and fulfilling a purpose.

Think about it: when you are the recipient of kind words, and actions, or share fun experiences, stress seems to melt away. The feelings of being overwhelmed by life recede. Anxiety eases, leaving you feeling healthier and happier. You might even feel *affirmed*!

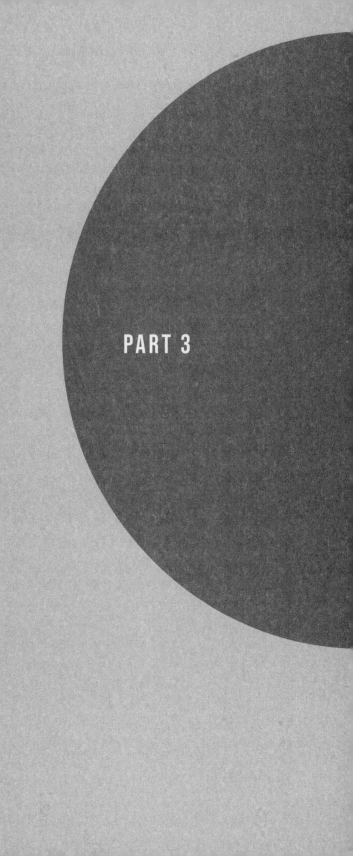

PART 3

CHAPTER 7

The Space-Between

Our friend and Safe Conversations leader Carlee Myers, founder of The Stress Less Company, recently told us about an experience she had with a coaching client with whom she had worked for two years. She helped the client, whom we will call Tom, make progress over that period, but when it came time to reenroll for another year with her, Tom said he had decided not to continue their sessions.

"I'm not signing up for this. I'm done," he told her. "I did the work for two years. I'm not doing any more."

Carlee said Tom's comments triggered her own insecurities at first. Her mind played out the lingering negative story that had popped up during times of stress, despite her years of success coaching clients one-on-one. That negative story was, *I'm not good enough, and what I offer is not of value.*

Carlee genuinely felt that Tom would benefit from another year of coaching, but before she talked to him again, she took the time to step back and look at the Space-Between her and her client—the space where her own insecurities existed and needed to be cleared out of the way so she could focus on what would be the next best step for Tom.

"There was a time in my business when I would have responded to him with a counterargument about why he was wrong to want to stop our sessions and why he needed to continue," she said. "Instead, when he told me of his decision, I just mirrored him and said, 'I'm hearing that you feel like you received everything you need from this program and there's no more room for growth here.'"

Tom listened and replied, "Well, that's not necessarily true. I know I just said that. There are things I want to work on, and there are things that I want to grow in."

Carlee said that their conversation then "became much more heart-centered." She and Tom were able to focus not on her trying to sell him on another year of coaching, but instead on what Tom realized was best for himself and his development.

"It's ultimately about connection. I think because he felt seen and understood in his fears and his vision, he ended up reenrolling for another year," Carlee said.

Clearing the Way

Like Carlee, most of us have emotional baggage—including the insecurities and negative stories we tell ourselves based on our experiences and personal histories—that can affect the way we react and interact with others.

This is a very common issue. If a teacher once told you that you would never make it as a lawyer, you might take that as a challenge to motivate yourself to get a law degree. Then again, if one day you have challenges in representing a client, you also may recall that teacher's words and think, *Maybe I'm not cut out for this profession, just like my teacher said.*

These lingering doubts and fears can either hold us back or motivate us to do better—and sometimes they can do both, depending on the moment. We all live from the past toward the future, and our brains are primed to anticipate that whatever happened in the past could happen in the future. All we need is for something to happen that triggers those insecurities. The goal is to consciously shut down the negative thoughts and focus on moving forward to create our best possible lives.

Carlee realized that her own narrative about not being good enough or providing enough value was triggered by Tom's initial decision to stop their coaching sessions. And our friend was wise enough to take a step back, acknowledge her own insecurities and their potential impact on her interaction with Tom, and then clear them out of the figurative space between them.

That Space-Between holds the baggage that can negatively influence how we communicate and relate to others—if we let it. Yet that space is also where positive memories and experiences exist. Your hurtful and your inspiring memories, criticisms, praise, failures, and accomplishments—all of these were created in that space between you and those with whom you interact.

By training yourself to recognize when negative memories and emotions—those that exist in the Space-Between you and other people—are triggered, you can shut down those that interfere with your ability to communicate and build relationships. And you can make the decision to tap into those memories and experiences that are more positive and productive.

As an experienced coach, Carlee was aware of her triggers and her insecurities, and she owned them. Before responding to Tom, she cleared out her baggage so that there would be nothing but a safe place to land for her and her client. As a result, they were able to focus entirely on what was best for Tom.

SC Dialogue provides a structure to keep the Space-Between safe for both you and those with whom you interact. It will help you keep from becoming reactive or defensive so that you can connect safely with others, just as Carlee did in working with Tom.

The Space-Between is the place where SC Dialogue can take place. You may be thinking, *Wait! Isn't the earthbound definition of space an unoccupied area? So how do you care for an empty space?*

The Space-Between you and your family, friends, coworkers, and other mortal beings may look empty, but there is a lot going on in there, including eye contact, voice tone, body language, and internal energy. In fact, the quality of your relationships is determined by how you take care of the Space-Between you and anyone with whom you want to communicate and interact.

Think of that Space-Between you and everyone else in relation to the spaces in the universe itself. When we look up at the night sky, we're looking into outer space. It was long believed that the Space-Between heavenly bodies was empty, but then astronomers discovered that powerful energy fields exist between them that influence what they become.

Outer space is filled with dark energy and gravitational pulls that hold up the massive planets, moons, and suns, rotating with exact precision in their orbits. It's the forces in the Space-Between that choreograph and maintain heavenly order in the universe.

The same holds true for the Space-Between you and those with whom you interact. Yes, it may be invisible, and it may appear to be empty, but this relational space is also replete with energy that determines the quality of your relationships with family, friends, coworkers, and anyone in your sphere. The fact is that your life takes place in the Space-Between you and everyone with whom you connect.

In our work, we view the Space-Between two or more people as an energy field. We agree with the saying that "everything is energy and that's all there is to it." So when we ask you to take care of the Space-Between you and other people, we're referring to the energy between you.

Our SC Dialogue focuses on this energy field. This is where the problems occur when differences arise, and it's where healing happens when you find ways to engage with others safely and productively. How you care for this space—this energy field—determines the quality of your relationships.

When you're in a dialogue with other people, there are really three entities involved: you, them, and the Space-Between. That space can unite or separate you and them. It can be filled with positive and productive energies that bring you closer, such as joy, gratitude, admiration, and appreciation. Or it can divide you if it is filled with negative and polarizing energies, like anger, critical judgment, anxiety, blame, and dark memories.

You can't see the Space-Between, so you might argue that it doesn't exist, but think about this: You can't see the wind, but you know it exists, right? Or what about the air you breathe but cannot see? When is the last time you saw gravity? But let go of your coffee cup and it's there, right?

Physics is all about accepting the reality of many things we cannot see, such as black holes, dark matter, and nanoparticles. There is a lot going on in our universe that we can't see, which is also true of our interactions and relationships with others.

We have all experienced situations in which we may have offended or angered someone because we said or did something that triggered negative feelings in them due to their own past experiences or opinions. Maybe you made a derogatory comment about a neighbor without realizing the other person was a friend of that person. Or maybe you asked a coworker to do something that the person felt was beneath them or not in their area of expertise. Unknowingly, you made them feel unsafe or insecure because of something you did not realize existed in the Space-Between you and them. This is because our connections go beyond anything we can readily comprehend.

The Space-Between is not a metaphor or a psychological construct; it is something that exists between all of us. It is ontological—an unchangeable feature of reality. You can influence the quality of the field and determine whether it is positive or negative by what you think, do, and say to others.

Following this concept, the combativeness and conflicts that seem to be more frequent between us are coming from all that negativity and triggering *stuff* that exists in the Space-Between us. You may become highly offended and angry with a fellow Rotary Club member who makes an offhand, snide comment about "illegal immigrants" because in the Space-Between there exists your own, more sympathetic feelings toward immigrants. The Space-Between is where your differences with your fellow club member exist, but it is also the space where you can find issues that you agree upon and even a place where you can help the other person find more sympathy and understanding on the immigration issue.

If conflict can be triggered during communications with others, then change and mutual understanding can occur in the same place. Life occurs in the Space-Between, and it is remembered in the Space-Within you. *Changing your inside world occurs when you change the quality and content of your interactions with the outside world.* The flow is from the outside in, then from the inside out.

Making Connections

Connecting with others is a basic human desire. Remember, we live in a connecting universe. Everything everywhere is connecting with everything everywhere all the time. Since we are made of the stuff of the universe, it is our nature to connect. That is why, without such connections, most of us feel lost and fearful. You might say we feel "lost in space," which is not a good thing. As the protective robot used to say when a threat arose in the *Lost in Space* television series: "Danger, Will Robinson!" When you are lost in that space, you feel adrift. Afloat. Isolated. Without purpose. Without meaning.

So to make safe and productive connections with others, especially those who might have different opinions or perspectives, we encourage you to think of that space as your place to reach out and seek to understand and to be understood, as well as to listen and be heard. To respect and be respected. To feel safe and to be perceived as safe.

The next time you feel someone pushing your buttons, threatening to make the conversation contentious, think of the Space-Between you and that person. Imagine clearing out all your insecurities and baggage from that space so that nothing that is said can stir anger or resentment in you. And then think of how you can make that space a place where you both feel safe and secure to discuss your differences and move forward despite them.

It may take a while to master that process, but imagine how helpful it would be to be able to talk to anyone about anything without rancor or hurt feelings. Changing the quality of the Space-Between is the only way to recover the sensation of full aliveness and joy—our original nature.

To understand how to communicate and relate to others,

you need to be aware of the quality of the energy that exists between you and those with whom you interact. You have two choices: you can make the Space-Between safe, or you can make it dangerous. If the Space-Between is safe, connection will be restored, and you will thrive and feel fully alive. If it's dangerous, you will instinctively feel defensive and will protect yourself. You cannot turn the danger sensors off, even if you want to.

You may not be aware of ways you evoke danger with others in the Space-Between. You may rush around, use a harsh tone, roll your eyes, and occasionally shame, blame, or criticize. These negative interactions trigger anxiety and activate defenses in those with whom you want to communicate and build relationships.

On the other hand, you can choose to make the Space-Between safe for the others in your life. You can use a kinder tone of voice, ask them how they are feeling, or express gratitude about something that maybe you've taken for granted. This respectful quality of interacting affirms others as valuable and helps build a sense of safety and trust.

Ultimately, the Space-Between is where you recover awareness and experience connecting. It's the quality of your interaction that opens opportunities for productive communication and lives of meaning and fulfillment.

Tapping into Your Brain Power

In recent decades, the field of neuroscience has had two breakthroughs relevant to the Space-Between you and those with whom you engage.

The first breakthrough was the discovery that our brains can rewire themselves and modify connections through a process known as neuroplasticity, which allows our brains to reorganize their structure and how they function.[1] In other words, our brains are always changing, which is why we can continue learning, developing, and forming memories throughout our lifetimes. You can help this rewiring process be beneficial by being selective of the thoughts you allow—or don't allow—to run through your mind.

The second breakthrough in neuroscience was the discovery that our brains are social—meaning they are shaped and reshaped by your experiences in the natural environment but also most profoundly in your relationships, especially with those closest to you. When you feel there is a threat, your brain releases neurochemicals, including cortisol and adrenaline, that create fear and anxiety. When you feel safe in the presence of another person, your brain releases dopamine, endorphins, and oxytocin, which are the neurochemicals of pleasure that make you feel warmly toward that person.[2]

The more you can create safety, caring, and humor in any interaction or relationship, the more productive and lasting it can be. To improve your communication and relationships, you might want to think about how you can trigger safe feelings in others to release dopamine, endorphins, and oxytocin in their brains. What words, tone of voice, or expressions would work best to accomplish that sort of brain bonding?

Another thing to keep in mind when creating a soft place to land with others is that energy follows attention. What you focus on is what you get. So if you focus only on the differences of opinion between you and other people, then you are probably triggering neurochemicals in your brain that are not conducive to productive discussions or lasting positive relationships.

We encourage you to look beyond differences for more positive things, to trigger the brain chemicals that will bring you closer rather than push you apart. Are you both parents? Then you have that shared experience to build upon. Sports fans? Jazz buffs? Avid readers? Horse lovers?

Focus also on the positive qualities of other people rather than dwelling on perspectives or opinions that differ from your own. What you look for is what you will find. If you focus on the good, your neural pathways will rewire, and those connections will help you improve your connections with others in the world around you. Tap into the power of neuroplasticity!

Shifting from Judgment to Wonder

Judging is something best left to professionals, including courtroom judges, line judges in tennis, and the celebrity judges on *American Idol* and *The Voice*. You don't want to judge others in the workplace, your organizations, or the community. It's time-consuming and, all too often, a trigger for conflict and aggravation.

Unless someone specifically solicits your advice or a critique of their performance, your judgment will likely result in a lose-lose. The person you judged will feel disrespected and threatened, and that individual's response will put you on the defensive. Meanwhile, the Space-Between will become a battle zone rather than a safety zone.

When you offer a judgment on someone else's actions or

performance, you take on the role of an expert or a superior, so you had better be at least one of those, and probably both, to go there. Being judgmental stems from the self-defeating attitude we discussed in previous chapters—the unwillingness or failure to accept differences between you and others. As we noted before, accepting difference is one of the greatest challenges we all face in trying to engage productively with other humans. Why? Because we are all imperfect specimens.

So how do you stop yourself from judging others and muddying up the Space-Between? We recommend dropping the know-it-all attitude and adopting the more humble and healing attitude of "not knowing." Not knowing is an amazingly liberating approach to life. It takes the pressure off having to know everything, which, you must admit, is a heavy burden even for brainiacs like Marie Curie or Albert Einstein.

You may know a lot about your profession, your business, and the organizations to which you belong. That's a good thing. But you cannot assume that you know everything about everyone around you—even those you think you know well. We think the best way to improve your relationships in general is to assume you need to know more about them, using curiosity rather than judging them.

In other words, to protect the Space-Between and keep it safe and cleared of toxins so you can have positive interactions and relationships, be curious, not judgmental. Ask questions instead of offering opinions. Rather than feeling compelled to express your wisdom or your judgments, embrace the concept of having a beginner's mind. This means that you approach every situation and every individual as if you are encountering them for the first time so that you make no judgments or assumptions; instead, you want to understand them.

Too often, we lose our capacity to be impressed, astonished, and awed by others. Becoming curious about the "otherness" of those in our circles and communities allows us to discover new things all the time.

Think of this as a permanent sense of wonder that nurtures positive communication and mutually beneficial relationships. The word *wonder* has two meanings: There is the verb form, as in, "I wonder what we'll do this weekend." There is also the noun form, as in, "I suddenly realize my coworker is a wonder to behold."

Every person has a galaxy within them—a reflection of their life experiences, knowledge, and talents. You cannot possibly know all that exists within the galaxies of everyone you encounter. So taking the attitude of not knowing is logical and less stressful than the alternatives.

Perhaps the best way to know someone is to "not know" them. Neuropsychiatrist Dan Siegel says that tolerating ambiguity (aka *not knowing)* is a sign of brain health.[3] It fosters creativity and helps develop your sense of wonder, which opens you to productive communication and positive relationships.

Wonder moves you beyond the stressful need to know everything, and in the process, it inspires you to be curious and seek understanding instead. This is good for your relationships because it helps you accept differences in others, rather than clashing over those differences.

Remember that difference is the defining feature of nature. When you embrace the differences in others, you open your life to new possibilities. They may also become curious about you rather than judgmental. We are champions of welcoming our differences with others to invite collaboration, cooperation, and cocreation into the Space-Between.

Our research suggests that a work environment where everyone feels connected and valued despite differences is conducive to greater productivity. Healthy relationships contribute to workplace satisfaction, a decrease in absenteeism, a reduction in medical complaints, and less conflict, plus an overall improvement of the bottom line for businesses.[4]

CHAPTER 8

Safe Conversations Work in Every Aspect of Life

We are often asked how SC Dialogue works in everyday life, so in this chapter we offer examples of our process being put to work in a wide array of situations and settings from around the world. They were compiled with the help of our many friends and associates who teach and practice SC Dialogue.

Connect and Have Safe and Direct Conversations

Let's begin with examples provided by Mo Byres of Dallas, Texas, who is a woman of many talents and interests. She is a life and recovery coach certified in Safe Conversations methods who does a lot of work with members of twelve-step programs.

Mo is also passionate about her sideline as a makeup artist, which feeds her artistic side. In addition, she is training to become a yoga instructor, and she often helps her husband, Tim, a James Beard Award–winning chef and restaurateur, by using Safe Conversations skills in his consulting business.

Mo offered compelling examples from her Dallas-based recovery coaching business, Instar Coaching; her makeup business, FGM agency; and from her private life as well. We have changed the names of her clients to protect their privacy.

Mo Byres's client Melanie began drinking alcohol at the age of sixteen and became a chronic alcoholic. She'd had a series of alcohol-related troubles over the years, including auto accidents and a one-night fling that resulted in pregnancy and a child.

Melanie had been in and out of alcoholism treatment and counseling programs beginning as a teenager. She was thirty-two when Mo began working with her as part of a team of psychiatrists and therapists trying to work through Melanie's family issues and help her finally stop drinking for good.

"We had these group sessions with her and her family, and it became clear that one of the problems was not *what* they talked about but *how* they talked about it," Mo noted. "I said that you need tools for talking to each other. The only safe place you can have a family dialogue is here. You need to learn how to do it so that you are not just spinning the same stories but getting to solutions instead."

Melanie had issues with her mother stemming from Melanie's childhood battles with cancer. Her mother, a loving woman, had devoted herself to helping Melanie but had become overprotective. Even after Melanie was cancer-free and into adulthood, her mother continued to be controlling in her daughter's eyes.

"Melanie didn't want to feel like she was still fourteen years old all the time," Mo said. "She felt her mother monitored her conversations with her son and did not trust her or think she was capable as an adult."

Melanie and her mother had trouble working through their issues until Mo introduced them to SC Dialogue. Following the SC Dialogue process, Melanie was able to explain to her mother that as a child, she understood she had cancer, but her mother usually excluded her from conversations with her doctors, which made her feel "managed and filtered."

"Melanie felt like, *I'm going to die, and I just want to hear the truth*," Mo explained. "She was fragile, but she wanted the truth instead of a version of it delivered from her mom. Once we began using SC Dialogue, they could speak authentically to each other about this historical event. Her mother had not known Melanie felt that way."

The mother, in turn, felt she was being blamed for Melanie's alcoholism, so she was put on the defensive in past conversations, and Melanie would get exasperated and think, *It's always going to be this way, so I might as well keep drinking.*

Melanie's mom was trying to protect her during her cancer journey, but Melanie just wanted to be heard. She felt that her mom didn't think she could handle the truth, which left her feeling insecure and lost and contributed to her alcohol abuse. As she grew older, Melanie felt her mom did not trust her and did not treat her as an adult because she was an alcoholic. And so the cycle continued.

Mo shared that with the help of SC Dialogue, Melanie and her mother were able to connect and have safe and direct conversations about this "huge pain" for the first time. "Melanie now feels her mom hears her when she talks about the pain of their disconnection, so Melanie can share her feelings without her mother getting defensive."

Melanie, who had been through alcoholism treatment nine times, now credits Mo Byres and SC Dialogue with helping heal her relationship with her mother and reclaim sobriety.

THE ORGANIC APPROACH TO SAFE CONVERSATIONS

Mo Byres has used Safe Conversations tools for so long in her coaching that she finds herself using it organically in every aspect of her life, including in her work as a makeup artist. She offered an example from a recent photo shoot for a Texas company's marketing campaign. The company wanted to feature photographs of its factory workers in the campaign. Byres was brought in to help them look their best for the photo shoot.

"Being in a makeup chair is very intimate. I'm in your personal space, touching your face, so I work at making you comfortable. In this case, these were regular people who were honored to be asked to appear in the photo shoot for the company, but some of them were nervous, too, so I worked to calm them down using SC Dialogue in an organic way to help them feel safe, calm, and happy. I listened to them and gave them affirmations in ways that many of them have never experienced, and they expressed how deeply touched they were because they had never been heard like I heard them," Mo said.

On-site at the Texas factory, Mo was working with an attractive young woman who seemed to be more nervous than most of her makeup clients there. "When I locked eyes with her, I felt her fear. I knew instinctively that there was something more going on with this woman when she sat down in my chair, and that I needed to go into intentional mode. So I was mirroring her and validating her to help her feel safe, telling her that I wanted to help her feel confident and pretty for the photo shoot."

Mo said she felt a connection with the woman. "We were sending and receiving information about each other, and I asked her if she was nervous because she'd never done anything like this before."

The woman responded that yes, she was feeling a bit nervous.

"She was a cute young woman," Mo said, "so I didn't think she was insecure or hung up about her looks. I thought it might be something else making her nervous. Remaining curious, I asked her questions to find 'the more.' Is the issue an internal or external fear? At one point, I asked her if she was happy with the wardrobe selection they'd made for her. She'd worn a short-sleeved shirt to work because they're required to wear them in the factory around the machinery, so I didn't expect that to be the problem. An expression came over her face that told me I had found the issue. When I looked down, I saw that she had a bad scar on her arm. I asked her if she was afraid of people seeing her scar in the photos being taken for the company brochures, and she told me she was.

"I promised her that we would help her with that," Mo said. "I didn't press for information on the scar's origins. That's her story to tell. I stopped asking questions because I knew what she needed. I validated her concern and empathized with her. She worked in a small-town factory where employees are very close, and I could tell she was comfortable with her coworkers seeing her scar. So I mirrored their empathy and told her we would make sure she felt safe and comfortable in the photo shoot.

"Once I told the young woman that I would share her concerns with the photo shoot producer so that her scar would not be noticeable in the photos, everything shifted! We rallied as a team so that during the shoot she was able to enjoy herself. She laughed and smiled and was adorable."

After the young woman left, the agent for the marketing company came up to Mo. She had been sitting off in a corner, working on her computer in the same room. "She asked me what I'd said to the young woman when I was doing her makeup," Mo recalled.

"When I asked her why she wanted to know, the agent said she saw a nervous young woman transform into a smiling, laughing, confident woman, and she wanted to know what I did." Mo told the agent about helping the young woman overcome her fears and nervousness about the scar on her arm by assuring her it would not be an issue in the photo shoot.

"Making her feel safe with the scar made me feel so good too," Mo said in reflecting on that experience. "I'm glad I didn't miss the moment or the opportunity to help her. What if she'd gone out for the shoot and everyone had gawked over her scar, or some lighting guy had asked her about it and embarrassed her? She didn't need that. I wanted her to feel loved and accepted by us, just as she was by her coworkers. Everyone has scars, and by using the SC Dialogue, I helped her get beyond what made her feel different from us. It's all about connecting."

THE VALUE OF CREATING SAFETY

The very next day, Mo had another opportunity to use SC Dialogue when the photo shoot team moved to another of the company's factories near Uvalde, Texas—scene of the 2022 mass shooting at an elementary school in which nineteen students and two teachers were killed and seventeen others were wounded.

"I was doing makeup for another young lady and using the SC Dialogue organically to make her comfortable when she just spilled out this horrific story," Mo said. "I realized that most of the people we were working with that day had children in that school, so I pulled the crew together and told them we had to be conscious of that delicate atmosphere we were working in."

Mo said that as the makeup artist, she is often the only person on a photo or video shoot who has the time to connect with people in a way that makes them feel safe and comfortable. "I am the connection point for most of them, and SC Dialogue gives me the skills to do that."

SEEK TO UNDERSTAND

The final story from Mo Byres comes from her personal life. Mo noted that she has taught the SC Dialogue process to her mother, who was born in Cuba but now lives with Mo and her husband, to help talk through issues that come up in their day-to-day lives. Recently, they used it to work out a common mother-daughter issue: doing the dishes.

"My mother says it makes her crazy to see dirty dishes piled up in the sink," Mo said. "So I asked her why she gets so insane about that. To me, she acts like I stole a thousand dollars rather than left some dirty dishes behind."

They went into SC Dialogue to explore her mom's feelings on the issue, and Mo realized it was more than a housekeeping issue. As a six-year-old in rural Cuba, Byres' mother was left for a long time with relatives when her own mother had to go to the city to get medical treatment for tuberculosis.

"When her mother came back, she found my mom had been neglected and was living in terrible conditions," Mo said. "She had lice and physical injuries, and my grandmother went off on the relatives for neglecting their important responsibilities to take care of her child and the place she lived."

By using SC Dialogue, Mo came to understand the history behind her mother's need to be in a clean and orderly environment. "She wasn't mad at me. She took it personally when she saw the dirty dishes stacked up because it made her relive something bad in her childhood. When we talked through it, I realized the impact it had on her. So now, even when I am rushing around because of work, I take five minutes to do the dishes."

Mo said she also texted her siblings who live nearby and told them, "The next time Mom is being weird about something, just remember that there's probably a story behind it."

Mo summarized her experience with SC Dialogue. "Being committed to using Safe Conversations as a way of life for all communication is like having a magic spell. Your friends, co-workers, family members, and so on absolutely don't have to know anything about it for it to work. When I allow myself to be safe for others (go into the curious space, pause and listen, mirror what I'm really hearing and not what I think they mean), I do feel empathy and want to validate their experience. They always feel it, too, and that's when the magic happens. No matter how difficult or complicated the topic is, it will work if you practice it. Start with the easy stuff and work your way up to the hard topics. It takes a real internal commitment to become the source of safety in order to create a Safe Conversation."

We all wish for total love and harmony within our families, but experience teaches us that sometimes the most contentious relationships begin at home with those we know and love but sometimes butt heads with.

Family Members Need Safe Places to Land

William, an accountant trained in SC Dialogue, had always been close to his cousin Danny, but their relationship deteriorated after Danny started dating a woman.

"We stopped talking," William recalled. "I know when you start a new relationship, you become a bit consumed. But this felt different from his past relationships."

After a few months of not talking, William reached out to his cousin, asking him if he had time to meet for a beer and talk about things. They met at their favorite pub.

William followed the process by starting out positive. He said to Danny, "You've been like a brother to me. And ever since you started dating Veronica, it seems you're avoiding me. We used to have a beer together, hang out, watch Sunday football. I'm not sure why we don't anymore. Did I do something to upset you or Veronica?"

William shared that his cousin didn't say anything at first, but then he got a bit teary-eyed, stood up, and hugged William. "Danny told me he needed to hear that. That he missed hanging out too." Danny shared that his girlfriend knew about their earlier "bachelor" days together and seemed threatened by that. "But he promised me that he would speak with Veronica and let her know that I'm like a brother to him and there's no threat there," William said.

"It will take a bit, but we have had a couple of family gatherings together. And I think Veronica is starting to feel a bit more accepting and less threatened by me, especially as her relationship with Danny becomes stronger."

Sometimes we think that if we didn't have family drama, there would be no drama at all. In fact, sibling rivalry has provided storylines for Shakespeare's *Hamlet* and *King Lear*, Fyodor Dostoevsky's *The Brothers Karamazov*, the battling Lannisters in George R. R. Martin's *Game of Thrones*, and most recently, the madly dysfunctional Roy family on *Succession*.

And yet, most of us want our family relationships to work, and that is why our SC Dialogue can be the most useful household tool ever created. Empires could have been saved if the Lannisters and the Roys had practiced even a little mirroring and empathy.

Safe Conversations creates a level playing field in conversations, where any topic can be discussed calmly, regardless of age, gender, or family roles.

Listening Inspires a Re-Marriage

With every relationship, there are stages, particularly when it comes to partnerships. Often, we forget why we were initially attracted and connected to someone. Safe Conversations helps us remember the person we first admired and recover that affection by listening with empathy and working to understand perspectives. This creates a sense of safety so you can let down your defenses, relate emotionally, and work on working out the important issues dividing you. This next example comes from a couple who attended one of our workshops.

Derek and Michelle had decided to file for divorce after ten years of marriage. Michelle said, "Things weren't too bad, but I was young and didn't have a mentor to tell me to stick with it. Co-parenting our son kept us connected, but also, our feelings never really died."

As sometimes happens, this couple started dating again after their divorce was finalized. They loved each other but needed a better way to work out disagreements and differences, so they attended our workshop. Michelle realized that she tended to shut down when conflicts occurred, keeping her concerns and feelings to herself instead of telling Derek how she felt.

For his part, Derek came to understand that his listening skills weren't as well-developed as he'd thought. He learned the difference between listening to someone while thinking about your own response versus listening to understand what the other person is saying and feeling. He also tuned up his approach to handling conversations about contentious topics. "When it comes to conflict, I tend to bow out gracefully. I don't want to add to the pain. That's why I granted Michelle the divorce she asked for, even though I still loved her. Now, with these tools, I know that I can share how I feel without adding pain."

Derek realized that building a relationship is a continuous process. He learned to trust that when conflicts occurred, he and Michelle could overcome them together. Michelle learned that as well, and she gradually allowed herself to be open with Derek about her feelings.

Two weeks after attending their first Safe Conversations workshop, Derek and Michelle remarried, which is about as good a result as we can hope for with couples who've come to us in search of healing.

As we stated earlier, we learned so much about bringing healing to relationships with couples that we expanded into all sorts of relationships and into communities and their educational, social, political, advocacy, spiritual, and governmental organizations.

Safe Conversations Goes to School

Many years ago, there was a *New York Times* number-one, bestselling book titled *All I Really Need to Know I Learned in Kindergarten* by minister and author Robert Fulghum. The basic idea of the book is that in our first year of official schooling, most of us learn essential things that stay with us the rest of our lives: Play well with others. Sharing is caring. Clean up your own messes. Look both ways before you cross the street.[1] While we agree, we would add another ten years or so, at least through middle school, as so much is happening to our bodies and brains developmentally, emotionally, and physically. It's during these early school years when we begin to navigate differences outside the family unit, often for the first time. We imagine a fourth *R* being added to the basic skills students are taught: Reading, wRiting, aRithmetic, and Relationships (okay, we took some creative liberty here!), hoping that teaching our SC Dialogue method for dealing with differences would serve them well for the rest of their lives.

We tend to have idyllic memories of our early school days; in truth, there are many lessons learned about dealing with life's challenges even in kindergarten. For many children, this first year of formal schooling is where they must learn to deal with a group of their peers in a structured setting. There are rules and schedules and other kids you must adjust to, including some who want what you have, or don't like you for whatever reason, or don't want to do what you would like them to do.

Young students are quick to adapt SC Dialogue skills, as they are helpful in negotiating relational challenges. Here's an example.

Two kindergarteners are having an epic battle over a coveted Pokémon toy in the classroom. After carving out time, the kindergarten teacher, Miss M. (MM), facilitates a Dialogue between the two boys, John (J) and Andrew (A).

MM: Andrew says that is his favorite toy and he didn't get to play with it all week.

J: Then you should've asked for it rather than push me!

MM: John says you should've asked for it rather than push him.

A: But I forgot to say all these words. That's why I grabbed it.

MM: You forgot to say all these words.

A: (*Starts crying.*) I want to be John's friend.

MM: You want to be John's friend.

A: And I barely have any friends.

MM: And you barely have any friends.

J: I'm your friend. I just wanted to play together with the toy.

MM: Did you hear that? John says he is your friend and that he wants to play together with the toy. Did you want to say anything else about pushing John?

A: I'm sorry.

MM: Andrew says he's sorry.

J: It's okay.

All parties hug. Issue resolved. Lessons learned.

So that's how SC Dialogue works in kindergarten. By sitting two arguing classmates on the floor facing each other, the expression of mirroring and empathy alone can model essential skills that get integrated into a young child's brain.

Instead of having the participants take turns as speakers and listeners, for the youngest of students, facilitators can take on the role as listener for both, mirroring and empathizing with words, facial expressions, and tone. Often, the children go off to run and play afterward. Sometimes they do stay sad, but they feel they've been heard and seen, and that helps.

Our SC Dialogue skills can help you talk to anyone despite your differences in every aspect of life, throughout your entire life.

Some Imago facilitators and Safe Conversations leaders have used the SC methodology and tools in the school system—from teaching kindergarteners how to manage reactivity to navigating conflicts between middle school students, guiding teachers and counselors to work with parents and students, and handling interpersonal conflict between colleagues.

In 2008, clinical psychologist and Imago therapist Meira Tamir was asked by the minister of education in Israel to help create a school manual that included various aspects of Dialogue. Every counselor in every school in Israel received this manual, titled *Teachers-Pupils Dialogue*, which included different dialogues for all ages with instructions. For ten years, Meira was invited throughout the country to give presentations about SC Dialogue—which were attended by headmasters, supervisors, teachers, counselors, and administrative staff—where she had audience members practice various scenarios. In turn, these folks went back to their schools, offices, and classrooms and practiced the essential skills.

A childlike wonder helps create safety and understanding. We teach all our clients, young and old-er, that when you practice wonder by asking, "Is there more about that?" you create a space where anxiety and defensiveness can't exist. Instead, a gateway to connecting opens pathways in our brains that unveil the pain underneath.

One colleague, who was also a guidance counselor, shared a time when she facilitated a SC Dialogue between a student and a vice principal. The student had snuck alcohol into a school event. While the vice principal was prepared to punish him with suspension, with the counselor's guidance, they shifted the conversation to 1) starting the meeting with an appreciation toward the student ("I appreciate your honesty when you took ownership for sneaking in the bottle of vodka. That took a lot of courage"), and 2) moving into curiosity ("Tell me more about why you felt compelled to bring this into the gymnasium").

After moving deeper and deeper between the mirroring and curiosity dance, it became safe enough for the student to ultimately share his chaotic home life and feelings of despair, which allowed the vice principal and counselor to arrange some support services.

When we move from our pain and blame, we bring an appreciation for our world so that safety and joy can be restored within our families and communities.

This shift from "knowing" to "not knowing" connects us on a heart level. This is our relational superpower. When Safe Conversations expands across all human ecosystems, we believe transformation follows.

Resolving a Conflict in an Alternative High School

John Castronova has a doctorate in school and clinical child psychology, and he has practiced as a mental health counselor for more than twenty years and is a certified Imago Therapist. He has needed all his training, knowledge, and experience as a principal in an alternative high school where, as he says, "Conflicts are prevalent."

John recounted an incident involving a student who was being disrespectful in class. Here is his story of using SC Dialogue in the very real world of an alternative high school:

The teacher contacted the social worker to come to the class to intervene. When the social worker arrived, the student was cursing and saying inappropriate things in front of the class.

When the adults tried to calm her, she escalated and refused to comply with the social worker's request, even though they had a strong connection and had been working together for most of the year.

The student eventually stormed out of the room and went to the main office. The social worker and teacher both submitted discipline referrals to me, following school protocol. This behavior would normally result in detention or suspension, depending on the severity of the incident.

I decided that I would prefer to do a mediation with the social worker and the student. It is my firm belief that discipline is a knee-jerk reaction and serves neither the student nor the staff.

I had the social worker and student report to my office for the mediation. I began by having them sit across from each other with me mediating between them. I first explained to them that we were going to talk, but there were ground rules for the way that they could communicate. I then explained the basic steps of the SC Dialogue process.

The student was the speaker first so that she could express how she was feeling, and the social worker could become the listener and mirror her statements. The student explained how she felt ganged up on and that triggered her. As the dialogue progressed, she shared that this is how she feels with her parents at home. It's them against her.

The social worker validated these feelings and empathized with how it must have felt scary to have two adults yelling at her.

When it was the social worker's turn, something incredible happened. She started out by explaining how it was for her to have the student be noncompliant, which the student mirrored. But then as the dialogue progressed, the social worker shared something personal about her childhood and how the student's defiance triggered some feelings in her.

The student was able to validate and empathize with her social worker. In a matter of fewer than thirty minutes, you could see how the bond between the student and social worker became that much stronger.

There was a mutual understanding of each other and genuine empathy. They each apologized for how they had acted and for having triggered the other. The results were greater empathy and taking responsibility for one's own actions for both the student and the staff member.

None of this emotional growth would have happened if the student was just given detention. And the SC Dialogue made it possible to implement this resolution seamlessly in a timely and efficient manner.

John seems to be the sort of thoughtful and wise person who is perfectly suited to the challenges of being a principal in an alternative high school. We salute him for his work and thank him for his story.

And now let's look at another dedicated and fearless practitioner of our SC Dialogue, a former police officer who decided to put our process to the test in an even more challenging situation.

Taking It to the Street

Clay Arnold is a former police officer who co-owns a life-coaching business with his wife, Sonja, a former educator. When Clay took a workshop on SC Dialogue, he was skeptical about how it would work in real-life situations, especially for first responders.

We can't blame him, of course. Police officers, firefighters, and emergency medical technicians deal with people in the most stressful of circumstances, often life-and-death situations. First responders never know how those they encounter on the job will react, and often, they have only seconds to put their training into action.

Clay decided to take our process to the streets to test it. Here is his story:

I initially did not buy into Safe Conversations Dialogue after taking a workshop, so I decided to put it to a test. As I was driving around one day in downtown Dallas, I encountered a homeless man who appeared to be having a psychotic episode— talking loudly when no one was around. I knew first responders dealt with this scenario all the time.

I began to have a conversation with him. He began talking to me while also having a conversation with his mama, who wasn't present.

The pivotal point was when I said, "Is there more about that?"

He stopped cold for a minute. "You really want to know more?" he asked.

"Yeah, I really do. You're a human being. You must be here for a reason. Tell me the rest of the story."

After this, I found out more about him. He had been on the streets since he was fifteen, when he was kicked out of his house. He'd been off medications for a year. He was mentally and physically in crisis. I did the whole process with him—mirroring, validating, empathizing—and watched him become calmer.

His tone began to match my tone. His whole countenance changed, lowering in intensity. People in his situation are not used to anyone listening to them. So our engagement in that moment was transformational for him.

He knew I was really engaged and was genuinely interested in listening. He probably had not had that sort of conversation in many years, if ever. This guy was around forty-five years old. He'd been on the streets all those years.

Our conversation went so well that we ended up going to get a hamburger together afterward.

Clay later talked about that experience and shared our process with other first responders, explaining that it could be used when dealing with people on the streets or with domestic disputes. He explained that SC Dialogue could be helpful to them in these ways:

- It de-escalates situations, including often-dangerous domestic abuse scenarios.
- You can attain more truthful information when you get people to use their frontal lobe (for reasoning) rather than the emotional part of the brain.
- You don't have to fix them or play therapist if you use Dialogue to simply talk to them.

Clay told us that the response from the police community to using SC Dialogue as a tool was "a very positive thing." He continued, "The SC Dialogue skills are a way to get around sounding like a therapist in difficult situations, which is helpful because there's a stigma to that. Police officers also have found mirroring helpful in decompressing stressful situations."

Clay has gone from being skeptical about whether SC Dialogue would work in the real world to using it in all sorts of ways, both in his personal life and even in working with his wife, Sonja, in their life-coaching business. They were creating an online course for couples, but Clay and Sonja had differing opinions about the content.

"We would just shut down because it wasn't working and

soon began feeling very frustrated," he said. "So we decided to go back and Dialogue about it. The process allowed us to find the source of the triggers that were causing difficulties. We wanted the same thing, but we came at it from different places. You forget that sometimes. And then we ask each other, 'Why did we waste two whole days fighting?'"

When people ask Clay and Sonja how they work together, they say: "We enjoy it, but we are also very different. This is how we are able to work together—by creating safety in the space to talk through our problems and frustrations."

Their son-in-law, who is an ER nurse, saw how well this worked for Clay and Sonja, so he decided to learn the SC Dialogue process to help him deal with the stresses of working in a children's hospital.

"He often came home distressed, but he didn't want to burden his wife," Sonja said. "He didn't want to feel like he was dumping his difficult experiences on her. They found that SC Dialogue offered a structure to share without anyone feeling like they had to fix his feelings.

"This was much better than simply not talking about his experiences, which would have led to keeping feelings inside and having to shoulder the burden on one's own. Now, he can share traumatic things, like the death of a child, in a structured way that helps him release the emotions inside while holding a relational space. This helps his wife to purely listen, validate, and empathize without feeling she either must solve it or become consumed by it too."

Clay also told us about using SC Dialogue with a teenage client who had "serious anxiety issues." This teen would "go berserk" when her father corrected her behavior by telling her to stop talking to people or to stop drinking sugary sodas. "She just wanted to be heard. The intensity of trying to fix her rather than hear her perpetuated the anxiety," he said.

To help the girl and her parents, Clay taught them the SC Dialogue process so they could listen to each other despite their differences. He reports that the teenager's grades improved dramatically when the family issues were resolved, and that she is now attending college and earning high grades there as well.

"She's learned how to regulate herself. She taught her friends how to use the SC Dialogue, too, and when she senses that she is feeling overwhelmed, she asks them to Dialogue with her. For her, it's been life-changing," he said.

Finally, we were especially moved by Clay's story of using SC Dialogue in communicating with his mother afflicted with Alzheimer's disease. He and his wife found it challenging when his mother moved in with them, but the couple said using Safe Conversations methods proved to be quite helpful.

"Mirroring her helped contain our emotions by providing structure for us all," he said, noting that his mother sometimes confused him for her brother, or her husband, and she often asked him to do things that were not connected to reality.

Again, SC Dialogue helped Clay keep in mind that there was no need to correct his mother or fix a situation for her, only to let her know she'd been heard. That was usually enough for her.

He offered this brief exchange as an example:

Mom: You really need to fire the cook.
Clay: Okay, so if I got that, I need to fire the cook. Did I get that, Mom?

If Clay had tried to correct her, noting that they didn't have a cook, or that the cook was doing a good job, it would likely have agitated her further. But by using SC Dialogue tools, he placated her. The conversation ended peacefully, he said.

Breaking Through

One of the wonderful things about creating our SC Dialogue process to bring together people of differing views and perspectives is seeing how it works in situations we never could have envisioned. So we will end this chapter with a compelling story from Jose Soto, a Safe Conversations leader:

I worked at a homeless encampment/safe-sleep sanctuary in the middle of the COVID-19 pandemic. I was responsible for welcoming people and supporting them in finding resources. I was encouraged to build a relationship with them and talk to them often. Guests slept in a parking lot in tents. Keep in mind that this was a low-barrier safe-sleep location. People were not asked to provide any IDs, and rules were kept to a minimum. Harm reduction was also practiced here, so guests were able to use drugs on the premises, such as fentanyl, crack, and marijuana. It was a high-stress environment.

There were many clients who had severe mental-health issues. I am not a therapist though. I was finishing a BA in family science at the time. There was one female client in her late forties who the staff had a hard time approaching. She would speak to herself out loud most of the time, sometimes yelling and screaming as if fighting with someone. Most of the time, if someone tried to talk to her, she would yell profanities in return. I knew that it didn't matter what the guest was going through. My first job was to listen, then mirror, validate, and empathize as much as I could.

Somehow, after several months there, she agreed to step out-side from her tent and speak a little more to me as I sat nearby. As she spoke, she stuttered a lot and was a bit jittery. She talked about how there were other women out in the streets who looked like her and committed crimes or did aggressive things. Because of this, people came up to her out of nowhere and yelled at her and mistreated her. But she was not the one doing those things. This made her life very difficult and unfair.

I listened attentively. I tried to communicate with my body language that what she was saying was important to me and that I was truly listening. Whenever I could, I would mirror, "So there are people out here who look like you. People confuse you for them and you get blamed for what they do. Is that what's happening?"

"Yes," she agreed.

"What else?"

I validated whenever it seemed appropriate with phrases such as "It makes sense that you're so upset. People are blaming you for things you haven't done."

I listened, mirrored, validated, and empathized for about an hour. After a while I sensed that she spoke more freely, and she even smiled at times. I also felt more relaxed.

On the way back to her tent, she offered me the best com-pliment she could have given me: "You know, no one has ever listened to me like that before."

We are still amazed by all the stories showing the real-world effectiveness of SC Dialogue, even though we have taught and practiced it for over forty years as therapists. More recently, we've taught it to the general public and trained persons from all walks of life to use it and teach it.

When people are seen, heard, and valued, you get the same outcome: people feel safe, share their feelings, and experience connection with friends, spouses, and strangers.

Although the SC Dialogue process is a new way to talk that has only recently appeared on the planet, we are confident it will become the language of most human beings. When it does, a new relational civilization will be born.

CHAPTER 9

The Power of Safe Conversations in Groups

After more than twenty years of applying our Imago Therapy methods to help couples heal and grow their relationships, we expanded our vision and our goals.

We wanted to use what we had developed and learned from working with couples to help entire groups of people.

The desire to expand our work to such a great degree was inspired, in part, by the horrendous, life-altering terrorist attacks on the United States that occurred on September 11, 2001. We felt all of humanity was threatened, and we wanted to help create a safer, more harmonious world in whatever way we could.

One of the results of our expanded work was the creation of an SC Dialogue tool for groups, which was originally called Communologue. This process was created by Imago therapists who used it in special social projects that interested them.

We decided to call it Group Dialogue because Safe Conversations will be largely used in groups such as corporations, educational institutions, houses of worship, and community organizations. The purpose of this tool is to help communities of all sorts use the SC Dialogue process and to allow members of groups to speak honestly and openly while exchanging viewpoints and perspectives with one another—even when they might have been contentious and ineffective in the past.

Most of us have experienced what it is like to be involved with groups that were rife with dissension, competing interests, and acrimony, whether it was a high school sports team, a college sorority or fraternity, a church group, a corporate division, or a professional organization such as the American Federation of Teachers, the American Bar Association, or the Teamsters Union.

There is bound to be some conflict in any group because human beings tend to have conflicting feelings and competing interests. And "objection to difference" shows up, sometimes, more intensely in groups that want to distinguish themselves from other groups.

Nevertheless, we are still the dominant species on this planet because, for the most part, we have figured out how to work together despite our differences. But we have a long way to go.

Although in the past, some members of a group would rather rumble in the streets than find common ground and rise above their differences, we think widespread use of our Group Dialogue tool will help us create a much better future in which we accept difference and celebrate the potential it holds for cocreating the world of our dreams. When done correctly, our process helps assure that speakers can safely express themselves and can count on their fellow group members to do their best to understand what they are saying.

With this tool, members of any organization willing to play by the SC Group Dialogue rules will feel safe enough to share everything. It provides a unique opportunity for large groups to move from entrenched conflict and distrust into a space where compassion, deep understanding, and free-flowing exchanges are possible.

"Imago theory is applicable to the workplace because of the influence of intrapersonal processes on interpersonal dynamics, which is the same influence that causes conflict in romantic relationships," wrote psychologist Amanda May Agathagelou in her 2013 doctoral thesis, which explored how she applied our methods with senior managers from the Lonmin Platinum Mine "to create understanding of intrapersonal and interpersonal dynamics to reduce the conflict levels they experienced in the workplace."[1]

Like Dr. Agathagelou, we believe Group Dialogue creates a space where problems may be solved, tasks may be accomplished or facilitated, and conflicts may be transcended. We know this works because it has been field-tested by our associates in our Imago International Training Institute. SC Group Dialogue can also be a holding space for group members to share an experience.

"It can be used for conflict resolution and healthy decision-making in large/diverse groups by utilizing the skills of dialogue, pre-validation, and safety for all perspectives. It becomes a process of not just cognitive learning, but also actually having everyone mirrored with no cross talk,"[2] said Rebecca Sears, a senior clinical instructor at the Imago Institute in Washington, DC.

We believe SC Group Dialogue brings three elements together to create harmony in any group: 1) safety, which is essential to connecting and communication; 2) respect for each person and what they bring, meeting our need to be seen, heard, and valued; and 3) hope where there may have been none before.

SC Group Dialogue follows these guidelines:

1. Establish a commitment to Zero Negativity in the meeting.

2. Ensure that the agenda, objective, time allotted, and people involved are set up for success.

3. Make an appointment in a one-on-one dialogue. This ensures that all involved are prepared and available to connect.

4. Share and mirror. Each member of the group shares their ideas about the topic. Their contribution is validated and captured in a central place.

5. Summarize.

Putting Group Dialogue to the Test

Here is a compelling, real-world example of Group Dialogue put into action.

In 2017, Hurricane Maria ravaged Puerto Rico and other islands in the Caribbean. The hurricane and its aftermath devastated the island's infrastructure, particularly its electricity grid and its communication systems, including internet service.

It took nearly eleven months to restore power to everyone, which made it the longest blackout in US history.[3] A research study later provided an estimate of 4,600 "excess deaths" by comparing the estimated post-hurricane mortality rate with official rates for the same period in 2016.[4]

The loss of cell phone and internet service was devastating for island residents trying to connect with one another and the rest of the world. After the hurricane, an international committee was formed to figure out how to restore internet service. Member organizations included Puerto Rican officials, the World Bank, the World Trade Organization, and the Institute of Electrical and Electronics Engineers.

After nine months of meetings, the committee members still had not reached a consensus on a plan. Beleaguered Puerto Rico residents were not happy, as you might imagine. We were invited by an associate who was the chair of the committee to come to Washington, DC, to help her with the committee meeting. Helen was unable to attend, but Harville was able to go. Just as the meeting was about to start, the chairwoman asked Harville if he would lead it, and he agreed.

The committee consisted of twenty-two members and a large group of spectators that included funders, donors, and a representation of social media wizards from Google, Apple, and Facebook.

At the beginning of the meeting, Harville explained the SC Group Dialogue procedures, guidelines, and nonnegotiables:

- Everyone who participated must follow the rules.
- Everyone's voice would be heard, mirrored, and valued.
- Members of the group would mirror each other and then ask, "Is there more?" And mirror until there was "no more."
- All matters discussed were confidential and contained within the group.

Harville then guided the meeting, continually reminding them of the Group Dialogue parameters. When members deviated from the rules, they were gently corrected. The participants came to respect the safe space that was created. In fact, two members of the committee offered their opinions and contributions for the first time, and their ideas were the most influential and convincing in the group. Being seen and heard led to impressive creativity.

After only two and a half hours, the twenty-two members established and unanimously signed off on a four-part summary and one-part conclusion for restoring internet service to the island of Puerto Rico. The impasse was broken, and the project went online with enthusiastic donors writing their first checks.

Several observers and attendees expressed their appreciation to Harville based on the success of his methods. They were amazed that this group, which had not agreed on a plan in nine months, had reached a unified resolution in under three hours. A standstill situation found direction and eventual success thanks to the powerful process. When asked how he did it, Harville simply said, "We created a safe space for everyone to be creative and engage in out-of-the-box thinking."

Opening Up Conversations and Improving Relationships

Organizational consultant and author Margaret Wheatley noted that "it is impossible to create a healthy culture if we refuse to meet. . . . But if we meet, and when we listen, we reweave the world into wholeness. And holiness."[5]

Our goal is for the new norm to become bringing together people of diverse opinions and viewpoints in various organizations. SC Group Dialogue creates a secure space in which the right/wrong or win/lose polarity is transcended and replaced by collaboration, cooperation, and cocreation. Every voice is heard, valued, and validated. Respectful speaking and respectful listening replace all forms of negativity—shaming, blaming, criticizing, or showing contempt—with mutual respect and cohesiveness.

Group Dialogue is also an open-ended process without an

inherent outcome or result, but it can, if the group chooses, prepare the ground for the group to reach a simple agreement or make a decision, as it did with the hurricane committee, through consensus or a ballot. It can also equip decision-makers to choose a direction that reflects the "mind" of the group.

Our widely applicable tool can be integrated into all of life's ecosystems.

- Community organizations can use it to integrate staff processes, cocreate solutions to community problems, and create cohesion between diverse groups that tend to polarize.
- Schools can use it for staff meetings, student organizations, and for teaching subjects in the classroom.
- Corporations can apply this process for corporate culture building, creative brainstorming, and decision-making.
- Congregations can find it helpful for small and large groups and classes to discuss differences in religious orientation.
- Families can use it for problem-solving, decision-making, and building cohesion.

Step-by-Step Overview

Under the guidelines for SC Group Dialogue, everyone is seated in a circle to eliminate any symbols of a hierarchy. All are encouraged to send short and clear messages. All speakers' words are mirrored, either exactly or paraphrased. Admittedly, this slows the process, but it also deepens the experience for all. Anyone can volunteer to do the mirroring or to share in it with other volunteers. Expressions of diversity are encouraged, but heated debate and negativity are discouraged. We encourage people to avoid statements that imply there's one absolute and objective truth. Parallel monologues are forbidden.

If a person wishes to respond with a thought or reaction rather than mirror, we ask that they convert their response into a positive statement and add it as another perspective to the emerging consensus of the group.

When silence occurs as a response to the emerging wisdom of the group, it should be allowed and honored. If there is a threat to the safe environment, sharing should be encouraged and carefully mirrored. Keep in mind that sharing without judgment creates unity within diversity and moves the group toward connecting and creativity.

Here is a step-by-step overview of SC Group Dialogue in which the group:

1. declares its commitment to be kind, respectful, and inclusive;
2. clarifies its intention by setting an agenda;
3. articulates its vision by expressing three adjectives that describe the desired outcome;
4. asks the facilitator to mirror contributions from members by making notes and posting them throughout the process;
5. selects a member to summarize the process and conclusions;
6. develops a consensus;
7. establishes a plan of action;
8. creates a timeline;
9. asks individuals to commit to take on necessary tasks

and complete them within the agreed-upon time frame; and

10. reconvenes at another time with tasks completed and continues its work within the Group Dialogue structure.

Safe Conversations and Group Dialogue in Liberia

We know that Group Dialogue can seem like an abstract concept, but when you put it to work in the real world, the results speak for themselves.

In 2021 and 2022, in partnership with the Foundation for Women, we brought Group Dialogue to Liberia as a community development and curricular tool for schools and school communities across that troubled country.

For fourteen years, from 1989 to 2003, Liberia was ravaged by a devastating civil war that resulted in the deaths of nearly 250,000 people. The warring forces raped and mutilated women and forced children to fight. Many Liberians fled the country to escape the chaos and violence.

Liberia was still struggling to recover from the civil war when it was hit with an outbreak of the Ebola virus in 2014. Even before the virus hit, the country had only fifty doctors for a population of 4.3 million. More than 4,800 died before the end of the outbreak in 2015. The nation's health-care system was further devastated by the loss of health-care professionals and the destruction of its supply chain.

The West African nation has now been at peace for two decades; however, it is still facing critical challenges due to poor health care, a lack of basic amenities, inequality, violence against women, corruption, and unemployment. The civil war, the Ebola outbreak, and then the COVID-19 pandemic have left Liberians vulnerable, as you might imagine. They have struggled with poverty, health challenges, and community fragmentation.

Deborah Lindholm, a friend of Helen's who has done philanthropic work in Liberia and many other places, asked us to do a Zoom workshop on Safe Conversations and Group Dialogue for the Foundation for Women staff in Liberia and 150 teachers and principals from their partner schools. Over the five-hour session, we taught the large group the SC Dialogue. In addition to the lectures, we put the participants in small groups to practice the Group Dialogue process.

We had an incredibly positive response to our Zoom session. The Foundation for Women team planned to take the program to their 450-plus partner schools across Liberia, with the eventual goal of reaching every school in the country. Deborah and her husband, Samuel Mayson, became certified leaders of our program so they could teach it themselves. In addition, a Dallas-based Safe Conversations Leader, LaSheryl Walker, was invited to Liberia to help teach the course. She spent two weeks there in August 2022, teaching in the schools. LaSheryl was interviewed by *FrontPage Africa* about her experience. Here are excerpts of her comments:

We were scheduled to have the workshop with the faculty and staff but there were many youth on site that day as they were out of school for their summer break. The students wanted to attend the work[shop] and I was impressed with their desire to participate. . . . It was so special to be in the room with them, to look at their faces, to see the smiles, the curiosity, and to make that connection in person. Seeing them one on one was moving. I was impressed with how well they really got the concept and how they were able to articulate what they learned back to the group. It was also nice to hear how they have been putting the skills learned via the Zoom workshop into practice. Many gave examples of how they used it at home, at work, and with their friends.[6]

Since some of the participating staff are connected to government officials, they developed the idea of taking our process and tools to the government, with the goal of making Liberia the first SC Dialogue/Group Dialogue nation and a model for elsewhere in Africa.

To further discuss this goal, Samuel Mayson was interviewed about the project.

As part of efforts to sustain Liberia's peace and security ahead of the October polls, the Foundation for Women (FFW), in partnership with Safe Conversations, a US-based organization, has embarked on a dialogue series called Safe Conversations, a new way that teaches citizens how to talk and approach issues with a sense of appreciation. . . . If practiced successfully, [Safe Conversations] will allow Liberians, despite their political and religious affiliations, to coexist. . . .

In an exclusive interview with the *Daily Observer*, Mayson also imagined how the world would be when everybody could come together and reach an agreement through Safe Conversations. "It will be a happy world where things will move smoothly. This is something that we anticipate if we use the Safe Conversations methodology. We will be fine."[7]

Other feedback has also been enthusiastic, even musical, you might say. To our delight, William T Yah and DJ Raw Mitchell, two Liberian men, produced the "Safe Conversations Awareness Song," which includes these lyrics written by William: *"Safe Conversations is all we need to solve all the people's problems in this world. If you have a problem with your friends, use Safe Conversations. If you have problems with your parents, use Safe Conversations. If you have problems with your family, use Safe Conversations. Because it is all we need to solve our differences in this world."*[8]

When they sent a video of the song initially, it was in rough form, so we asked if they could produce it in a studio, which they did, and it's wonderful.

Liberians who have learned our process understand that Safe Conversations and Group Dialogue can help heal the divisiveness and trauma residents have endured for so many years.

And we're not stopping with Liberia. We also meet regularly on Zoom with partners teaching our SC Dialogue process in South Africa and Nairobi, Kenya, and in churches, schools, and universities. We have learned in Africa that our SC Dialogue tools can be useful in any culture to help anybody talk about anything to anyone, despite their differences.

Revitalizing a Community Agency Through Group Dialogue

Al Turtle, a skilled practitioner of Imago Therapy, retired a few years ago as a psychologist and relationship therapist in Idaho, where he was celebrated for his work in the community as well. When he stepped down as a board member of the local United Way of Kootenai County in Northern Idaho, for example, it was noted that he had volunteered more than 150,000 hours of his professional time to the organization.

Al was an early adapter of Communologue/Group Dialogue

and used it for the benefit of his local United Way. He was known for helping people feel safe and comfortable in conversations, even if there were differing views in play.

For example, Al was asked to meet regularly with a group of Army Reserve–enlisted men and their noncommissioned officer leaders who were not getting along because of trust issues and, as a result, had difficulty completing their work. By using SC Group Dialogue methods, he enabled them to develop mutual respect and trust and begin working together effectively.

Al was also known for his work as the facilitator of meetings of the local United Way's board of directors, where he made it safe to express differing views through "pre-validation," a process based on his belief that "everyone has in their mind a personal rationale for whatever they say, and that's OK."[9] He also used mirroring and other SC Group Dialogue methods to let members know that they were being listened to and understood. His facilitation methods ultimately helped to bring more dynamic leadership that revitalized the organization.

Bringing Together Historic Enemies to Increase Understanding

There are few groups in modern times with a history of conflict like that of the Israelis and Palestinians, whose contentiousness traces back to the end of the nineteenth century. The Hamas attack on October 7, 2023, brought this history to a horrific level in our times.

Before that already infamous attack, several organizations, companies, and everyday people brought Israelis and Palestinians together peacefully—seeking understanding, connection, and solutions. The indiscriminate attacks on civilians, however, justifiably caused feelings of rage, despair, betrayal, fear, and revenge, resulting in large-scale destruction and trauma throughout the region. At the time of this writing, the question of survival is too real for both Israelis and Palestinians (and unfortunately for Jews and Muslims around the world).

We decided to keep the following story in the book, despite the events that began on October 7, not only to honor the legacy of the work in Israel by Imago faculty member Orli Wahrman, but also to remind us of what is possible. And while reconciliation, healing, and peace may seem profoundly remote, we remember that the same was true at one point for people traumatized under apartheid in South Africa or during the civil war in Liberia or for the countless other nations ravaged by war. Safety, however, is indiscriminately an absolute. Without safety, SC Dialogue is not possible. Thus, with Orli's blessing, we share the work that was done in Israel prior to October 7.

World-renowned Imago faculty member Orli Wahrman, a native of Israel and a pioneer in implementing Communologue, has endeavored for years to bring Palestinians and Israelis together through Group Dialogue.

Encouraged to bring positive change in the world, Orli conceived and led the Palestinian-Israeli Imago Project from 2002 to 2008, and was also involved in the Jewish-Arab Co-Existence Group, which began in 2006.

When this dedicated peace activist first conceived of bringing Palestinians and Israelis together, she led a demonstration workshop with two Israeli and two Palestinian couples in her private clinic, with support from the Israel Trauma Coalition. A Palestinian partner joined to provide equal representation and sensitivity to cultural differences.

The workshop was deemed a success, which allowed her to

secure a $50,000 private grant to launch the peace project using Group Dialogue as the process for overcoming entrenched differences between the twenty-five rotating Israeli and Palestinian couples.

She established with them that the goal of using Group Dialogue and its trained facilitator was to create an environment for the safe sharing of personal viewpoints between two groups that might otherwise be unable to tolerate each other's views, combining couples' work and Group Dialogue, or Communologue, into a beautiful holding container. The participants agreed in advance to follow the process guidelines throughout the sessions.

Their first major Peace Project workshop was held in Istanbul, Turkey, to create a neutral ground and reduce political distractions. Five Arab and five Israeli couples came together for the four-day workshop. After the initial two days of a couples' workshop, they were encouraged to discuss any subject in the peaceful Communologue process. All participants were considered equals.

In their early discussions, the differences in their cultures became clearer than ever, Orli said in an interview later.

> We Jews learned that the traditional Arab society is a men's society. Socially the conversations are between men. Men hang around with men. Wives in Arab couples are not normally treated as equals. The dialogical approach to relationships was quite new for them and full of potential. A second and wider form of equality came as both sides learned about life stories. Once we got down to the painful issues behind our present quarrels, we found out how similar we really are.[10]

The participants were not the only parties to learn from the workshop. The leaders also had to be flexible in their approach due to cultural sensitivities. This included even changing common metaphors used in workshops, such as "crossing the bridge," which reminded participants of checkpoints common in their disputed territories.

"Telling them to go to a safe place brought a reaction that for them, there is no safe place," Orli noted in an interview with Donald L. Gibbon. As a result, "We had to change our texts to make them more appropriate."[11]

Even when the workshop participants and leaders went out to dinner at a Turkish restaurant, the history of conflict followed them—and yet, so did their experiences with Group Dialogue. When other Arab diners asked the Palestinians why they were sitting with Israelis, they answered, "They are our friends!"[12] After the success of the Istanbul sessions, several other meetings of the group were held, including one in Haifa, far from Jerusalem and overlooking the Mediterranean Sea. For this session, Arab participants were guests in the homes of Israelis, which was a major cultural challenge because many Arabs would consider that to be sleeping in the home of a traditional enemy.

The Arab participants came away from that experience with a different view of their hosts. It was noted that their hearts and views of Israelis may have softened and opened a bit. Some revisioned the soldiers at the hated checkpoints might be the children of their hosts.

Reports said relationships were permanently altered for participants on both sides. In fact, a family workshop was held in which children and grandchildren of participants were invited. Forty-eight people took part. The final session taught the children Imago principles, which bonded them all.[13]

Orli noted that the intense and violent historic conflict between these two very different participating groups resulted in many tense and emotional moments in the workshops, but the Communologue process rose to the challenge and kept everyone safe.

The volatile topic of Israeli withdrawal from the Gaza strip resulted in some especially tense exchanges in which the Jewish participants were not appreciative of how painful the occupation was. An Israeli participant validated by saying, "It's like somebody putting a knife in your neck, then, when they take the knife out, they want you to say, 'Thank you.'"[14] Thankfully, both sides stayed with the format—listening, mirroring, and offering empathy to overcome differences and advance mutual understanding.

The Lebanon War was another contentious topic during a session held after the last war in Lebanon in 2006. Hezbollah had been shooting missiles in the north of the country and the Israeli participants came to the meeting feeling traumatized. Orli said of the Communologue process:

> [It] helped us contain Palestinians saying that on one hand they cared about us and were thinking about us, but on the other hand they were glad that we got it. Everybody was crying, but we managed to listen without exploding. This is the power of this work. We also learned that they respect Hassan Nasrallah, secretary-general of Hezbollah in Lebanon, and we became curious to hear more. When you start listening, you learn all sort of stuff. Instead of focusing on who was right, we listened to discover and understand and put judgment aside.[15]

Despite some personal challenges in recent years, Orli continues to work for peace between these longtime adversaries through Group Dialogue. In an interview, she said: "We've kept our promise to them of safety no matter what. We've discovered a dialogue process for enemies or at least that our friends may have an enemy part in them. Couples and children are not a threat. We are able to talk to all of our people."[16]

As Orli has demonstrated time and again, Communologue (Group Dialogue) empowers participants to move from entrenched power struggles into compassion, deep understanding, and a free exchange of ideas.

After the Hamas attacks on October 7, 2023, Orli was completely devastated, traumatized, and heartbroken from the terrible atrocities done by Hamas to the Jewish Israeli people and the war that followed in Gaza. As we completed this book, any hope for peace and the possibility of SC Dialogue and Communologue seemed remote to Orli and to many others.

Orli is one of our heroes. Her successful and brilliant work with various cultures is a testimony to the power of SC Dialogue in transcending differences. She and Al have shown that SC Dialogue is powerfully effective in helping individuals and groups achieve safety and move toward connecting. Each time this happens, we have the makings of a transformed culture locally, and eventually a new civilization where peace reigns.

CHAPTER 10

Safe
Conversations
at Work

Maddie is a lead engineer UX web designer in the corporate office of a financial services company in Florida. She is also the mother of a two-year-old daughter, Nichole. Her husband, Kyle, is a project manager for a large software-development company.

Both worked at home during the COVID-19 pandemic. They hired an in-home babysitter to help with Nichole during working hours, and it worked out well. Now, Maddie's employer is trying to gradually bring its IT team members back into the corporate headquarters at least a couple of days a week. Kyle's company told him that he will not have to return to the office, which is fine with him since he had at least an hour's commute in heavy traffic.

Maddie has secretly begun searching for a job that allows her to work from home full time. Mostly, she believes she is more effective and less distracted working at home. Yet top management at her company has made it clear that they want all employees to return to the office eventually. She and the head of IT have discussed this and occasionally clashed over it.

Her IT boss says remote workers in general tend to have more conflicts and disagreements with supervisors because they rarely meet in person, communicating instead by texts, emails, Zoom, and other digital means that make it more difficult to build a sense of teamwork and trusting relationships. These challenges have become quite common in the postpandemic world of work, according to a 2021 study:[1]

- "Eighty percent of remote professionals have experienced workplace conflict."
- Forty-six percent use a work messaging app for their arguments.
- Nearly two in three workers (65 percent) have faced conflict with their coworkers. Nineteen percent have experienced conflict with their direct manager, 11 percent with an external manager, and 5 percent with an employee who worked at a different company.
- The cause of conflict came from a "lack of transparency/honesty about something important," according to 18 percent of respondents; 9 percent said it was due to a "clash of values"; and 2 percent said a "false accusation" caused the conflict.
- More than one-third of respondents (36 percent) "felt that their bosses were too aggressive in their texts."
- After enduring virtual conflict with a coworker or a boss, 39 percent of respondents said "they wanted to leave or actually left their jobs due to the problem."

And yet, those corporations where most employees have returned to their offices are also experiencing high levels of conflict over remote-work preferences. The major points of contention include:

- staffing issues due to the Great Resignation;
- generational gaps as younger workers replace those who have resigned and clash with older coworkers due to different values, issues of respect, and other cultural matters;
- communication problems often involving misinterpretation of texts and emails;
- differing attitudes about work and commitment to the job; and
- ill will toward the corporation, often due to layoffs, terminations, outsourcing, and compensation disparities.

Safe Conversations: A Path to Healthier and More Profitable Corporate Cultures

Many businesses recognize that healthy relationships and a sense of safety in employee communications are critical to success. Yet most businesses don't know how to achieve this.

Your company may achieve excellence in all other areas, only to be defeated by a toxic work environment. Why is it hard for employees to sometimes get along with one another and with supervisors and top managers?

A large part of the problem is, as we indicated in an earlier chapter, the traditional focus on individual achievement by the "best and brightest," the practice of monologue and objection to difference, and lack of awareness that healthy relationships are essential, not optional, for healthy organizations and the emotional and mental health of individuals.

This emphasis encourages competition rather than collaboration, and it tends to reward those who are the most aggressively ambitious rather than those who thrive by building relationships and welcoming diverse opinions. American business culture also traditionally has valued improving the bottomline short term over building relationships and empowering teams to achieve success over the long term.

For many corporate employees, the goal is to reach the top of the organizational ladder by beating their competition up the rungs. Their aim is to dominate the competition through self-promotion. The competitive spirit can also interfere with healthy work relationships, which in turn impacts a company's success.

By teaching people to talk without criticism, listen without judgment, and connect beyond differences, our SC Dialogue can help build a new culture in the corporate workplace. Happy employees in a healthy environment also improve the economic bottom line with increased profits.

Incorporating SC Dialogue strengthens teamwork skills and shifts the corporate culture so that employees and supervisors share a feeling that they are all in this together, working toward the same goals and sharing in the same rewards.

Adopting an open and collaborative work environment means people will feel more comfortable sharing their ideas and excited about carrying them out. This makes every employee feel heard and valued, which results in happier, more fulfilled, and more productive team members. Even better from a business perspective, the resulting free flow of ideas fosters creativity and innovation.[2]

The relationships between corporations and their employees,

between employees and their supervisors, between employees and each other, and between employees and their customers and clients are critical to the well-being of corporations everywhere.

A 2023 Gallup report said, "After trending up in recent years, employee engagement in the U.S. saw its first annual decline in a decade—dropping from 36% engaged employees in 2020 to 34% in 2021. . . . Active disengagement increased by two percentage points from 2021 and four points from 2020."[3] The respected analytics and advisory company also reported a "six-point decline in the percentage of employees who are extremely satisfied with their organization as a place to work. These are all indications that employees are feeling more disconnected from their employers."[4]

The Gallup report also noted that the largest decline in employee engagement was among those in remote-ready jobs who are currently working fully on-site. "It's worth noting that exclusively remote employees saw an increase of four points in 'quiet quitting,' (aka not engaged in their work and workplace)."[5]

Positive social interaction plays an essential role in employee well-being, which increases employee engagement. Engaged employees "exhibit more altruistic behaviors by providing coworkers with help, guidance, advice, and feedback on various work-related matters."[6]

We all want to have positive relationships with our bosses and coworkers. Who needs the stress of a toxic work environment? We would rather feel like our supervisors and coworkers share the same goals and support each other, right?

A workplace culture where everyone feels valued and supported is also good for business. Employee turnover is one of the most formidable invisible enemies of growth. High turnover rates disrupt corporate culture and weaken the fiscal health of the business. A public relations firm's survey of four hundred large companies found the cost of disconnection and poor communication from bosses and among employees was $62.4 million annually. The toll of failed business relationships can include loss of valued employees and failed hires, as well as broken partnerships, disgruntled stakeholders, and lost customers.[7]

Strong relationships with employees, partners, suppliers, investors, and customers are critical to economic profitability for businesses. Disconnections in the workplace can influence employee well-being and engagement, not to mention turnover and the bottom line.

Many corporate workers have told us stories of how they struggled in their careers because of communication and relationship issues with coworkers, bosses, clients, or customers. Maybe you and your boss had differing views of your responsibilities, and you couldn't come to an agreement. Or maybe a customer was unhappy with you and there was nothing you could do to resolve the issue. These are real-world problems in need of real-world answers, now more than ever before.

A Process That Works in the Real World of Work

After first learning the SC Group Dialogue process during the pandemic, Dr. Robin Hills decided to experiment with the elements of the SC Dialogue in her personal encounters with coworkers upon her in-person return to the corporate office. She found the way to a better relationship with one particular coworker through utilizing our SC Dialogue tools.

This is her story:

Mary was a fellow director of another department with whom frequent collaboration was critical to achieve the company's goals. Now, we have all encountered colleagues with this challenging personality type—easily offended, frequently complaining, blaming others, always right. One of the habits Mary had developed was to enter my office or those of my direct colleagues to vent about a decision or action made by our department.

My colleagues and I had many discussions about Mary's habit of "dumping" her complaints about other people and departments on us. It obviously made her feel better, but she often left us feeling stressed because the solutions to her complaints were beyond our control.

One day, I decided to try the "sharing a frustration" method of SC Dialogue with Mary right after she had left my office after making one of her typical complaints.

I walked over to her cubicle and asked if I could have an appointment: "Is now a good time to have a conversation about a frustration I have with you?" She agreed, and I proceeded to succinctly share my frustration about how her method of communicating her complaints stressed us out and put us on the defensive. I noted that the way she unloaded her frustrations also threatened the collaborative dynamic that we had been intentionally cultivating with her department since returning to the office after the pandemic. I asked her if she would be willing to learn the SC Dialogue skills.

Surprisingly, Mary, for the first time that I could remember, didn't defend herself but simply replied, "Sure, I can see that, and I won't do it anymore."

My colleagues and I were incredulous. Of course, this was not a magic fix. This is the real world, after all. But using the Appointment Process to engage her attention before expressing my frustration gave Mary time to focus and listen. And she apparently felt safe enough that she did not have to defend herself. And Mary did stop coming to our offices to complain about something we had no authority to change.

Robin's conflict with Mary was nothing earth-shattering. The conflict didn't affect the stock price of the corporation or threaten the company's bottom line. Or did it? If you were to multiply it by the hundreds of thousands of corporate employees around the world, maybe on a macro level it would.

We chose this example not because it is exceptional, but because it is all too common. Everyone who has worked for a corporation or large business has had similar experiences with a coworker or supervisor who made their workdays more stressful. And it is symptomatic of the challenges and issues that plague far too many corporations in modern times.

As a *Forbes* magazine contributor noted: "Failed relationships in business have high costs, both financial and emotional—expensive golden parachutes, failed hires who waste costly training, partnerships and investments that lead to misery and conflict, investments that make you wish you had put your money anywhere else, buyouts that lead to the destruction of a business you've nurtured over decades."[8]

When Robin engaged Mary in an SC Dialogue, she took a brave step to improve a workplace relationship with someone who was alienating her and her coworkers and unknowingly causing them stress.

We think our method helps make conversations like this safe and improves relationships in corporations, and it can do the same for anyone looking for a more collaborative and productive work environment. It's a simple solution to a profound challenge: talking without polarizing. Anyone can learn it and do it.

The Problem of Divisive
Relationships in Corporations

Many businesses today acknowledge the critical importance of healthy working relationships between employees at every level as well as between employees and customers, suppliers, stockholders, and other key persons. This is a step in the right direction, but most corporations do not know how to achieve that. Many companies have strategies for achieving excellence in most other areas, but not for changing a toxic work environment marked by competing interests, personal animosities, and divisiveness.

Corporate culture can be notoriously cutthroat. True benevolence has always been rare in big business, of course, but it is difficult to cultivate loyalty and a team spirit when employees live in fear of massive layoffs and terminations designed to appease stockholders. Skyrocketing compensation packages for top executives at companies in relation to wages for the workforce is another source of aggravation and frustration. The Economic Policy Institute, in discussing the fact that CEO pay has increased by 1,460 percent since 1978, noted that "corporate boards running America's largest public firms are giving top executives outsize compensation packages that have grown much faster than the stock market and the pay of typical workers, college graduates, and even the top 0.1 percent."[9]

From our work with businesses and their employees, we have observed that when the focus is on competition, not collaboration, little is done to cultivate mutually respectful, healthy working relationships. Dissension and contentiousness in the workplace have a negative impact on performance. We've found that many leaders struggle to find ways to foster teamwork and cooperation.

Team Success Is Rooted in Psychological Safety

In 2012, Google launched Project Aristotle, an initiative to study what made some teams of employees more successful than others. They found that a working environment in which team members could freely share their ideas and experiences made them more productive.[10]

We all want to feel heard and seen, not rejected or criticized, when we express our opinions, suggestions, and concerns in the workplace. It's that simple. Like most of us, you probably have more enduring memories of being put down or ridiculed by a boss or colleague than any recollections of praise or support.

Brain chemistry is the reason we tend to remember the slams more than the plaudits in our lives. When someone takes a verbal shot at you, your body triggers higher levels of cortisol, which sends you into self-preservation mode. This makes you more sensitive and reactive so that you tend to exaggerate the criticism and its negative impact. The effects of a rush of cortisol can last more than twenty-four hours, so your memories of being disrespected tend to linger.[11]

Supportive comments and encouragement produce a different chemical reaction—the release of empowering hormones—that opens you and makes you more communicative, more collaborative, and more trusting. It is one of nature's cruelties that the effects of this feel-good hormone don't last nearly as long as those of the hormones that trigger negative emotions.[12]

When a conversation feels safe, the brain releases dopamine, acetylcholine, and norepinephrine—what our grandchildren might describe as nature's own "chill pills"—which are neurochemicals that give you a sense of peace and calm. They also strengthen the immune system. Thus, a positive work environment leads to healthy employees who get sick less often.[13]

When you can share your thoughts without fear of judgment, you are more likely to bring your all and do your best at work. Teams, too, function best when everyone listens and remains curious, knowing they will benefit from these practices when it is their turn to speak. Psychological safety makes all this possible, and Safe Conversations is a tried-and-true skill that helps organizations achieve it.

James is an upper-level manager in a Fortune 500 company with more than fifty thousand employees around the country. He has worked there for more than twenty-five years, starting just a few years out of college, and served in several different divisions. Here are some of his insights into the importance of Safe Conversations and empowering relationships in the corporate world:

Throughout my career, I have learned a great deal about leadership in a corporate environment by observing both good and bad examples. On the negative side, I have experienced situations where I did not feel comfortable sharing my thoughts and opinions because of the environment set by leadership.

I specifically recall being requested by a senior leader to participate in a governing body alongside many people I'd had relationships with for years. We were provided the intent and goal of the group and told to "make it happen." There was no input, no feedback, no defined strategy. We were just supposed to make it happen.

This resulted in a toxic and tense environment in which certain dominators controlled the discussions and interactions. They made the decisions and there was very little collaborative discussion. The leadership of this group enabled this dictator-ship. This group included some very bright and experienced individuals, but because it lacked inclusiveness, their efforts were a waste of time and money.

I had witnessed other team members being berated by the dominators, who were, in fact, their peers, simply for asking questions or making suggestions within the group. Meetings became flogging sessions for those whose ideas differed from the dominators. There was no psychological safety. The intent and goals of this group were not met. It was disbanded due to over-whelmingly negative feedback about the lack of inclusiveness.

On the positive side, my experience with dominators on teams has informed my own leadership methods. My first course of action when leading any team is to establish one-on-one relationships with each team member so that I get to know them.

We share our personal backgrounds and interests as well as our goals and bucket lists. This really sets the tone, and it helps me understand their motivations and aspirations, as well as how I can best lead and coach them. In subsequent meetings, I open with questions like "How are things at home?" or "How was your daughter's recital?" The goal is to relate personally and authentically before we talk about work, to create a bond built on empathy rather than relating on a transactional level based on an approach that says, "What can you do for me?"

Building sound relationships and demonstrating your open-ness to being vulnerable with those you lead, or coach, goes a long way. We are all human and we all have faults and make mistakes. Through my leadership journey, I have learned that it humanizes my relationship with my team members if I am open and willing to be vulnerable, sharing my own faults, mistakes, and what I've learned from them.

I have had the opportunity to build or rebuild teams, some of which were underperforming because of these dominating individuals shutting out others. Developing an atmosphere of inclusiveness, in which all team members are instilled with a sense of belonging and feel valued, is a challenge all leaders face in the corporate world. And it is becoming even more challenging in remote-work environments where we get very little actual face time interactions among team members and those we lead.

I have found relationship building only happens if leadership enables it by supporting and practicing inclusion and diversity. This requires leaders to be active, unbiased, and intentional listeners with each person on their teams.

Leaders must do more than "hear." They must connect and provide total attention (no distractions) acknowledging what they are hearing by reiterating or summarizing back to team members what they've said to demonstrate that their input has been received and registered.

Active, intentional listening and mirroring must be backed up by action, not just lip service. Leaders must provide support to their team members by responding to their input with behaviors. This is critical because it establishes the all-important trust factor. People will not share or speak up if they do not trust the environment in which they work. It's all about relationships with the leader and with peers.

I believe leaders need to create and foster an environment where every voice is heard without disruption. My experience is that team members who feel supported and valued—and whose diversity of thought is welcomed—become very effective and efficient. This takes effort and time to instill and uphold.

Everyone in the room should be allowed to speak for an equal amount of time without interruption. This sets expectations and ensures the dominators do not control team interactions. I've found that dominators become frustrated and will leave if they aren't allowed to always control the agenda.

Yet, when I coached and fostered equal time for all in meetings, I've also had dominators thank me for opening their eyes to the value of diverse voices. Teams that do not build relationships among all members do not flourish and often fail to meet goals because of all the competing individual agendas at play.

I expect my team members to take risks, innovate, make mistakes, learn from them, and get better. At the same time, I want them to feel safe enough to share their mistakes and failures and what they have learned with me and even with the team. The team environment should allow this "psychological safety" of sharing thoughts, ideas, and even failures among all team members. The entire team benefits when one team member learns from failure and feels safe enough to share the experience.

James has not been trained in our Safe Conversations process, yet he has instinctively developed a very similar approach for leading teams in his corporation. And though he has had many years of experience in that world, James has learned to welcome feedback from all of his team members. He is an advocate of servant leadership, which is marked by openness and humility.

We are big advocates of this approach, which recognizes that "not knowing" is a powerful tool in corporate cultures seeking to improve communication and relationships in the ranks.

We know that not knowing goes against most strategies for success in today's corporate environments. When was the last time you heard a top executive declare, "I really don't know the answer to that question!"? (If you can't answer *that* question, it's okay. Trust us.)

So why should you pursue this counterintuitive strategy of

not knowing? Because it facilitates healthy relationships, and healthy relationships are good for business. Entrepreneur, author, and business strategist Dan Prosser has noted that companies in which employees practice collaboration rather than competition are 400 percent more profitable.[14]

Not knowing is a powerful tool for connection because it opens you up to the people around you, fostering mutual respect and strengthening your ability to collaborate and innovate with others.

Overcoming the Power Differential

Barbara was dreading her annual review with her boss even though she was confident in her overall performance. The "power differential" she felt particularly during her review was intimidating.

"I typically armor up for these meetings with confidence on one side and, on the other side, a commitment to saying as little as possible to get it over with as quickly as possible," she noted. "But this time, I decided to try using SC Dialogue skills. I figured, at minimum, doing so would increase my comfort level with the meeting."

When she met with her boss, Terry, for her review, Barbara took the initiative. She attended to the Space-Between them to help make a safe connection by sharing an appreciation.

"You know, I don't know that I have ever said this, but I want you to know that I appreciate you as a leader and mentor," she said.

That simple statement took the tension out of the air, put them both more at ease, and opened the door to a productive conversation. Terry got down to business, first sharing her strengths followed by two areas where Barbara could improve her performance.

"I agreed that I needed to improve in one of the areas but questioned the other area Terry identified," Barbara said.

In the past, Barbara might have become defensive, but rather than break the safe connection and positive mood that had been created, she again applied one of our SC Dialogue tools.

"Instead of defending myself, I mirrored their statement, repeating what I heard. I asked if I'd understood correctly, and if there was anything they wanted to add," Barbara recalled.

Terry welcomed this new, more positive approach by offering more of their perspective, shedding light on why they thought Barbara needed to work on these two areas to improve her performance even more, and stating the rationale. Again, Barbara avoided being defensive and respected Terry's assessment, simply saying, "That makes sense."

Throughout the rest of her review and afterward, Barbara felt much better than she had during past review meetings with Terry.

"Terry and I were connecting and relating with positivity. I am grateful to have a boss with the wisdom to ask what they can do to help me be successful in my position at the end of the review."

When Terry opened the door for Barbara to provide feedback, she took the opportunity to share a frustration that had been painful to her and her colleagues since they began having leadership huddles during the pandemic. Terry often would offer criticisms of individual participants with the entire group present.

She told her boss: "It would be really helpful to me if you would defer any critique of me or any of the members of the leadership team that arise during the huddle to a more private moment after the meeting. Praise in public; censure in private."

It was Terry's turn to be defensive, which Barbara anticipated, so again she put our Safe Conversations skills to work.

"I gently put my hand up and requested that Terry temporarily refrain from defending themselves and instead just tell me what they had heard me say," Barbara reported. "Yes, it was a very bold move on my part, but I believe it was appropriate in this private setting. As you'd expect, it did take them aback a bit, but they did mirror what I had said—just as I had done—giving me the space to provide additional rationale and explain specifically how such criticism in front of my peers makes me feel embarrassed. Terry understood and expressed they would try to avoid directing individual criticism during the group meetings."

And so, with the assistance of SC Dialogue skills, Barbara's annual review ended with both participants finding opportunities for improving their relationship without acrimony, fear, or resentment.

The Benefits of Safe Conversations at Work

Safe Conversations strengthens your teamwork skills, which is an increasingly valuable asset in the corporate world. This process for talking with anyone about anything helps you shift away from an individualistic mentality to one of collaboration, cooperation, and cocreation.

Companies that embrace the tools of Safe Conversations report that it encourages an open and collaborative work environment where team members feel more comfortable sharing their ideas. Creating a work climate that encourages safe and open conversations boosts brainpower and makes for more engaged and motivated employees who are better able to perform their duties and excel in meeting their goals.

Safe Conversations creates the conditions needed for employees to tolerate ambiguity and navigate even difficult and tense conversations at work. Our colleague Dan Siegel, an expert in interpersonal neurobiology, argues that tolerating ambiguity is a sign of brain health.[15] It allows us to experience differences of perspective and opinions without succumbing to the fight, flight, or freeze impulses we tend to experience when we feel challenged or out of our comfort zones.

When you are comfortable with ambiguity, you can appreciate rather than fear those who have differences with you. The prefrontal cortex is the area of the brain that allows us to tolerate ambiguity in this way. One of its functions is to help us pause before reacting, meaning we can resist the urge to respond immediately to the stimulus of a new experience and instead to react in a measured and thoughtful way. It is also the part of the brain responsible for neural integration, making it critical to mental and emotional health.

When you follow the SC Dialogue steps, you tap into that part of the brain that empowers you to accept criticism and differing opinions without anger or insult, viewing them instead as opportunities for growth and mutual understanding. You must admit, this is a much healthier approach to dealing with communication and relationship challenges in the corporate workplace, right?

We believe the practice of SC Dialogue helps employees reach their full potential and, by extension, companies will see improvements in their bottom line. Employees and managers with strong interpersonal skills will lead the way to a healthier, more collaborative work environment.

Women, especially, stand to benefit from that sort of work environment. Despite tremendous advances in recent decades, women still face significant barriers to advancement in the corporate world. They often feel like their opinions are not taken seriously and their contributions are not valued as much as those of their male colleagues. Safe Conversations provides a conversational structure wherein everyone's voice is heard and honored. It also provides a safe space for employees to convert frustrations into requests. In this way, it improves gender equity one conversation at a time.[16]

A final benefit of practicing Safe Conversations in the workplace is that it opens the door to innovation. If you are set in your ways and insist that everything be done in a specific manner (your way!), then you close yourself off to learning new and better ways.

Not knowing, working with a beginner's mind, and practicing will take you to a new level of thinking and achievement. Listen with openness and curiosity rather than with judgment and critical thinking. This will open you up to unconventional thinking, spurring creativity and innovation. Practices of wonder are a rich source of new ideas and, as a result, can lead you and your corporation to contribute to society in exciting new ways.

PART 4

CHAPTER 11

Healthy Brains

Safe Conversations Dialogue can help you have productive conversations and empowering relationships with anyone in any aspect of your life and career, despite your differences. But did you know that practicing the Safe Conversations skills can also contribute to a more relaxed and healthier brain?

"Having nurturing relationships is protective of mental health and overall brain health," said psychiatry professor Dr. Jennifer Gatchel.[1] In past centuries, scientists thought our brains did not change over the course of our lives, but they've changed their minds about that. (There's a joke somewhere in that statement.) Now, neuroscientists believe our brains are organs that can and do change—and that how we choose to think and speak is a part of that process.

Our conversational skills help us overcome differences with others so we can build healthier and more productive relationships that, in turn, boost our brains with calming and stimulating neurochemicals. So using SC Dialogue seems like a no-brainer, right?

We think, write, and talk a great deal about the brain because we spent a lot of time conferring with neurobiologists while creating our Safe Conversations relationship skills. We learned that the thoughts that run through our brains can change the way we feel. If we want to be angry, we think of something that ticks us off. If we want to be joyful, we think of something that makes our spirits soar. It's that simple.

This knowledge helped us save our marriage back in the early days. We were fighting often. We had gone through five therapists; we fired four, and the fifth fired us! She called us "the couple from hell." Can you believe that?

Things were not looking good for our marriage, but then Helen read a book on feminine epistemology and the brain, and a light bulb went off in her head.

"We don't need to get divorced. We just need brain surgery!"

Actually, what she meant by that was that we needed to get better at managing the thoughts and feelings we were running through our brains so that the words coming out of our mouths brought us closer together instead of driving us apart.

Over time, we became brainiacs, avid students of the brain and all its complex workings. Encased in silence and darkness in our thick skulls, the brain is like an inner universe. Though it weighs only about three pounds, the average brain has eighty-six billion neurons and works as our all-important control center for every human function.[2]

We found it fascinating when, a couple of years ago, two Italian scientists—an astrophysicist and a neurosurgeon— published a paper on the similarities between the network of cells in our brains and the cosmic web of galaxies in the universe. They came to see the brain's neural network as a universe itself, comparing its billions of neurons to the billions of galaxies of the universe: "The tantalizing degree of similarity that our analysis exposes seems to suggest that the self-organization of both complex systems is likely being shaped by similar principles of network dynamics, despite the radically different scales and processes at play."[3]

Train Your Brain

As complex and fascinating as it is, the brain's basic job is to keep us alive. To do that, it can change to reorganize itself by forming new neural connections, a process known as "neuroplasticity," which we touched on in chapter 7. This discovery—that our brains can be changed through our conscious efforts—is very empowering.

This means that by managing our thoughts, reactions, and behaviors, we can strengthen our cognitive and rational abilities. You can do this with the help of Safe Conversations skills that allow you to communicate with curiosity, empathy, and mutual respect. In the process, you create safety in your relationships and calm in your brain.

Safe Conversations can work as a daily exercise for improving your relationships, which improves your emotional well-being, your physical wellness, and your brain. Our process gives you the ability to harness the power of neuroplasticity.

To train your brain, you must focus on positive things, including problem-solving and goal-setting, instead of negative things like frustrations and setbacks. *What you focus on is what you get.* You may have to think about that twice to get it: what you have is a function of your choice. This is why expressing appreciation and converting your frustrations into requests is so important.

When you feel safe in your conversations and relationships at home, at work, and in the world around you, it enables your brain to foster positive social engagement, nurturing, and growth. Without safety, the flight, fight, or freeze response takes over, mobilizing the body and brain to respond to danger—whether the danger is objectively real or merely imagined.

When danger threatens, your brain sends out a distress signal. This prompts your adrenal glands to release a surge of hormones, including adrenaline and cortisol. These toxic neurochemicals make you upset, anxious, and angry. Your brain responds by telling you to fight, flee, or shut down.

If your lower brain perceives something as dangerous, whether it really is or not, the danger alarm goes off because your imagination is as powerful as anything that is real. For example, if a loud sound wakes you up at night—even if it is just a car backfiring outside on the street—the neurochemicals start flowing, and your body goes on full alert because your imagination takes hold and churns out possible worst-case scenarios. *It's not a backfire; it's a gun fired at my window! Grab the kids and pets and hide!*

Remember: Your brain is wired that way because for hundreds of thousands of years, it was shaped in an environment where there was no security, and it could not afford the luxury of not expecting the worst when something unfamiliar happened. And it still works that way.

The dangers in your corporate office may not be as life-threatening, but if you think your supervisor gave you a mean stare or ignored your request for a meeting, then you likely will perceive that as a threat to your livelihood, and your brain and body will go on alert.

Safe Conversations skills can help you overcome those feelings of distress so that you feel safer and more relaxed, which enhances the ability of your upper brain to fully function and your lower brain to stand down from its danger mode. This allows your body to release relaxing endorphins: dopamine and serotonin. These neurochemicals make you feel safe and relaxed, and then you are open to differing views. This helps you communicate and build healthier relationships, which, in turn, enhances physical and mental health, and creates a happier life.

When you feel seen, heard, and valued, your need is met, and you feel loved and peaceful, or love and peace. When this need is *not* met (for example, you feel invisible, ignored, and devalued), you feel heartache.

While the 2.8-pound organ in our skulls is considered by neuroscientists to be the most complicated organ in the universe, we simplify the science by teaching that the brain has only two parts: the Crocodile Brain and the Wise Owl Brain.[4] Our more playful names are not taught in medical school, of course, but maybe should be just to make it more fun.

The Crocodile Brain

If you allow your thoughts to stay in the lower part of the brain, you spontaneously release neurochemicals that are toxic and make you feel bad. When a person talks to you and you don't like what they say, your Crocodile Brain can become activated. You begin to think things such as:

- *I totally disagree with that.*
- *They are wrong.*
- *I'm smarter than they are.*
- *They better change their minds or I'm leaving.*

The function of the Crocodile Brain is to keep us alive and defend us from harm. So if it senses danger, it will respond with fight, flight, or freeze. These are built-in mechanisms to protect us when we perceive danger (whether it's real or not). We freeze if we hear an unexpected bang in the next room. We have a knee-jerk response if someone jumps out from behind a door. We run when we see a car speeding toward us. These responses often bypass our conscious processing. They are automatic.

During the majority of their day, crocodiles float quietly in the water and remain still, unless lunch swims by. Out of the water, they snooze on the riverbank, seemingly placid and harmless. However, if a bigger croc threatens them, or another threat appears and makes the crocodile feel anxious or threatened, it will spontaneously snap. Likewise, when engaging your Crocodile Brain, a feeling of anxiety or a perceived threat will make you spontaneously snap.

The Crocodile Brain does not distinguish between physical and emotional harm. A snide remark or a critical response will produce the same survival-based cortisol that evokes a defensive behavioral and emotional reaction. It can bite your arm off. A ticked-off crocodile is dangerous to be around!

The Wise Owl Brain

Practicing the SC Dialogue rescues you from the Crocodile Brain mode and invites you to think, feel, and operate from the neocortex, which we call the Wise Owl Brain mode. When you respond to what a person said by tapping into the SC Dialogue skills, the sentence stems take you into the upper brain. There, you are more thoughtful and intentional, so you respond with sentence stems such as, "Let me see if I got it." Or, "I think I heard you say

_____. Did I get it?" And, "Is there more?" Rather than reacting from the lower brain, you can use Safe Conversations sentence stems to check to see whether you heard the speaker correctly. This puts you squarely in your brain's neocortex.

Let's imagine you're having a conversation, and at this point, you're not agreeing with what the person said. They might be 100 percent wrong. But before you decide that, you first mirror what they said back to them to verify that you heard them accurately. Being heard calms the speaker and they feel respected because you are taking the time to check the accuracy of what they said.

When you mirror someone, you escape the negative energy of the Crocodile Brain and an unproductive my-way-or-the-highway attitude. Instead, you operate from the Wise Owl Brain and tap into curiosity rather than self-righteousness. You then can pick a time to share your point of view thoughtfully and respectfully. When you operate out of the Wise Owl Brain, you get the added benefit of releasing beneficial neurochemicals that provide a sense of calm, peace, and curiosity.

The Wise Owl Brain is capable of helping you control your inner crocodile. The wise owl can outthink the crocodile. The Wise Owl Brain organizes data, problem solves, and looks for more creative ways of doing things. It responds calmly and wisely. It looks for opportunities to collaborate, cooperate, and create a win-win outcome.

The Wise Owl's Upper Brain

When utilizing the upper brain, people tend to gravitate toward a particular mode of processing, a dominant way to think and look at the world. Some people lean toward reasoning, order, and logic.

They function similarly to a computer in that everything must add up, so they are good at creating structure.

Other people gravitate toward the visual, emotional, creative, and intuitive functions. They are good at seeing the big picture and can spot how different perspectives can intersect in various ways. They also tend to trust their gut instincts. They may not know how they know something, but they do.[5]

When it comes to having good relationships, you need to tap into all parts of the upper brain. Some people naturally are very good at one or the other. But when you use SC Dialogue, you tap into the rational mode by using skills like asking for an appointment to speak, by mirroring, and by asking for confirmation that you've understood the person correctly.

When you say, "Is there more about that?" and you listen to the other person's reasoning, you will become empathic with that person, tapping into the emotional and intuitive functions. Thus, when you use the Safe Conversations process, you integrate parts of the upper brain.

The challenge is to make sure your Wise Owl Brain is always in charge. When talking with someone who has views that are different from yours, you want to keep your Crocodile Brain penned up so your Wise Owl can swoop in and manage the conversation thoughtfully and without rancor. Your Wise Owl Brain is unleashed when you use the SC Dialogue skills. Safety, which is created in relationship, is what enables our brains to engage in SC Dialogue. Without safety, the fight, flight, and freeze responses take over (whether the danger is real or imagined) and we further polarize into isolation. But when we employ the Wise Owl, we create safety in the Space-Between and are able to become curious, discover the other, and grow beyond our differences. At this point, we can experience deep relaxation and joyful connecting.

CHAPTER 12

Healthy Relationships

Let's revisit how our process and skills work in the real world of the modern polarized, pressurized, and stressful work environment, which is marked by contentious conversations and relationships perched on a razor's edge. Many people wonder each day if they are walking into work or a hornet's nest whenever they get on a Zoom call or enter the corporate office.

Using the SC Dialogue process will improve your ability to achieve goals with individuals and teams. We call this achieving "relational competency," which is the ability to interact successfully with others by engaging and connecting beyond your differences.

Roberto

Roberto was working at home when he got on a Zoom call with the vice president of his employer's IT department and all the team members, most of whom were also working remotely.

As the vice president began the meeting, Roberto's dog, King, began barking at the Amazon deliveryman, who was dropping off a package. King's bark sounded like a lion roaring to everyone on the call.

The boss was not pleased. He went off on the team in general, and Roberto in particular, about the lack of Zoom etiquette in recent meetings. "We have dogs barking, people wearing T-shirts, women without makeup, and some of you appear to be working in your closets, laundry rooms, or bathrooms," the vice president complained. "I don't want to see your drawers in a dirty clothes hamper or your collection of heavy-metal band T-shirts, people!"

His rant went on much longer than King's barking. The vice president was on a roll. He proceeded to rip into nearly everyone on the team, claiming they were not performing up to expectations. After it was over, the IT team members turned on each other. There was a blast of blaming emails and texts back and forth, fully loaded with all the most polarizing and volatile ammunition of the times.

Roberto took more shots than most. Some suggested that he should turn in his resignation or turn King into the dog pound. There were political shots fired. Racist shots. Sexist shots. Cheap shots too. One person questioned Roberto's citizenship status.

Does any of this sound familiar? There must be a better way for us to communicate and relate to one another at work, at home, and in our communities. Our SC Dialogue skills are that better way. They help you improve your listening skills, enhance your levels of curiosity and wonder, elevate your sense of safety, and contribute to a healthier and happier life.

Leslie

Let's drop in on Leslie, a rising star in a large tech company. Leslie is ambitious and hardworking and increasingly frustrated because of her direct report supervisor, Walter, who is always anxious and seemingly under the gun due to his inability to schedule, plan, and complete his own projects.

He and Leslie have very different perceptions about what her daily duties and responsibilities are in her current position. Leslie applied for the job and was hired based on her perception. She has tried to explain that to Walter, who nonetheless insists on giving her projects that are not at all related to the job she was hired to do.

Leslie believed Walter was always dumping his projects onto her because he was incapable of completing them himself. She made a case for that with her department vice president, who agreed with her and instructed Walter to stop handing off his projects to Leslie.

Walter did not stop doing that. In fact, he did more of it. They had several volcanic outbursts over this issue. Leslie had reached the point where she began to perspire and shake whenever Walter came near her. She was having difficulty completing her projects with all the added work Walter dropped on her.

Their working relationship and conversations had deteriorated so much that Walter had begun using one of Leslie's staff members, Kay, as an intermediary. Leslie admired Kay for her ability to deal with Walter. She watched one day as Walter gave Kay a project that Leslie knew was not within Kay's area of responsibility.

She listened and marveled at their exchange.

"Kay, I need you to take over this project with the software team," Walter said.

"Walter, you look so dapper today," Kay replied. "Now, let me understand this. You want me to take on this new project while I am working on another project that is due next week? Is that what you're saying?"

"Yes, but you don't have to start on it until you've completed the other project next week."

"Okay, and, of course, you realize that this project requires special training and expertise that I do not have, correct?" Kay said.

"Oh, I wasn't aware that you didn't have the training and expertise for this," Walter said.

"Well, I would like the opportunity to move up to that level, so if you would approve it, I can sign up for the training and courses that will make it possible to do this sort of project in the future," Kay said. "Of course, that would also mean I'd move up to a higher pay level, which would be great. Will you sign off on that, Walter?"

"Yes. I mean, I think I can do that. Let me check with Mr. Henderson, the vice president of our division," Walter replied. "In the meantime, just focus on the project you need to complete next week."

After Walter walked away, Leslie pulled Kay aside.

"I predict you will be vice president of our division and maybe CEO of the entire company," Leslie said. "You handled Walter like a champ. I want to be you!"

Kay obviously has a high level of relational competency that helped her communicate without rancor with Walter, who walked away from their exchange feeling like he'd been heard and respected, even though Kay essentially rejected his request to take over the project.

Relational competency has that power. It helps you develop healthy relationships that can become transformational rather than transactional. Healthy relationships connect you to the greater experiences of life, the transforming power of wonder, and set you up for new opportunities for personal and professional growth.

Safe Conversations Process
in Your Everyday Life

You can become relationally competent by choosing to use the Safe Conversations process in your everyday life. This process includes dedicating yourself to improving your listening skills so that you listen to understand others accurately, and it opens up your mind through curiosity and wonder. This triggers activity in the healthiest part of your brain, which contributes to better physical and emotional health and happiness.

A seventy-five-year study at Harvard University found that good relationships are more important for our happiness than either money or fame. A research team that followed a graduating class of upper-class students from Harvard and a middle-class group of students from Boston University concluded that, irrespective of social class, close ties to friends and families can delay mental and physical decline and are bigger factors in building long and happy lives than social class, IQ, or even genetics. "The surprising finding is that our relationships and how happy we are in our relationships has a powerful influence on our health," Robert Waldinger, director of the study, reported. "Taking care of your body is important, but tending to your relationships is a form of self-care too. That, I think, is the revelation."[1]

Decades ago, we noticed this happening with our therapy clients who came in to talk about their problems. We assumed they were having emotional or thought problems, or perhaps work-related concerns. As they talked about their anxieties and fears, we noticed a pattern in how they managed their anxiety by turning it into anger and/or depression, or back and forth. When we kept trying to understand their depression or anger, each shifted to talking about their relationships.

From this, we realized that behind their obvious symptoms lay a deeper anxiety. They felt that they were not valued in their relationships, and that was the cause of the suffering. As the Harvard study found, relationships were what they wanted, and this emerged as the primary concern.

Clearly, our happiness and success are rooted in our connections with those around us. When relationships fail because of divisiveness, contentiousness, or poor communication, we often struggle in our careers and our social lives. The most important relationships are those with our family and loved ones. This is why repairing ruptured ties often starts at the roots of our families, the smallest—yet mightiest—unit of our global civilization.

Sadly, too often, when couples don't see, hear, and value each other, they grow apart, their families struggle, and a breakdown occurs, sometimes with painful and tragic results.

Listening to truly understand those around you, being curious about them, and responding with wonder draws others to you. They will want to have social interactions and engage with you, despite any differences you may have.

A relationally competent person practices the sentence stems of SC Dialogue at every opportunity. For example, in developing relational competency, you might offer sentence stems in an informal way: "May I share my thoughts about what you just said?"

Another example: "Let me see if I understand you correctly." Or, "Is there more to what you're saying? It's so interesting."

You also practice this skill by committing to Zero Negativity in your conversations and all your communications, and by offering affirmations whenever possible, such as, "I really like the way you expressed that thought."

Relational competency, then, is practicing SC Dialogue as a structured process, using sentence stems spontaneously while avoiding negativizing, and offering affirmations on a regular basis. The idea is to learn to love others equally, if not more than you love yourself. This will help you nurture unconditional acceptance and love toward anyone, despite differing views and opinions.

Embracing Relational Competency and Changing Our World

The Safe Conversations process is unusual in two ways. While being a relatively simple process, it is profoundly transformational. We've had people tell us that if taught widely, our process could work to treat and heal mental illness and maybe prevent it in many cases.

Adrienne Kennedy, an education researcher and mental health policy advisor who chaired the national board of the National Alliance on Mental Illness, took Safe Conversations training and became an enthusiastic advocate. She believes that healthy relationships are essential to personal well-being—both physical health and mental health. She thinks SC Dialogue skills—learned and practiced—have the capacity to guide us with simple, precise steps for building healthier, stronger relationships, which in turn provide the platform for better brain health, physical health, resilience, and joy.

The Institute for Emerging Issues at North Carolina State University recently recognized the crisis of disconnection and polarization and developed a program called Civic Conversations to encourage diverse students and members of the community to "spend time together in real and rich conversation in which all listen first to understand. Such conversations across differences are all too rare amidst the rising rancor and deepening division plaguing society. But we seek to make them the norm in North Carolina."[2]

The institute's laudable goal is to reconnect people across the state so they can learn from one another, build relationships, and identify opportunities to bridge divides. Similar programs cited by the institute included Better Angels, "a national citizens' movement to reduce political polarization in the United States by bringing liberals and conservatives together to understand each other beyond stereotypes."[3]

More and more, individuals and institutions across the country and around the world are realizing the need for such programs, because the failure to work through conflict and reach agreement or resolution has a negative impact not only on couples and families, as we've noted in other books, but also on our social interactions, our business relationships, and on our governments and their ability to function effectively or to work with other nations.

In a world of Safe Conversations, we believe politics would become far less polarized and contentious. Instead, we might return to Aristotle's intention of friendship. The philosopher believed the best friendships are "virtuous friendships" in which we become better together. In his ideal form of friendship, the primary focus is living good lives together; friendship is not about getting things done or having a good time but simply for helping each other become better and lead fulfilling lives. Virtuous friends celebrate each other's successes, and in hard times they comfort and counsel each other, and also tell each other the truth.

Aristotle wrote, "In poverty and other misfortunes of life, true friends are a sure refuge. The young they keep out of mischief; to the old they are a comfort and aid in their weakness, and those in the prime of life they incite to noble deeds."[4]

The philosopher wanted us to understand that "friendships are the building blocks of a society and, in addition, he is helping us understand that the building and dissolution of friendships is a natural process that contributes to the growth of a society—and this is a natural part of being human," noted Anika Prather, professor of classics at Howard University.[5]

We believe that Safe Conversations processes and tools can help to create more virtuous friendships and productive relationships that move us all into the next step of human evolution. We plan to share Safe Conversations in every language so that it is used everywhere to create connected communication and relationships that bring together people from diverse backgrounds and perspectives.

Choosing How to Communicate

Here is another real-life example of using Safe Conversations skills to deal with a conflict in the workplace.

A supervisor, Steve, approaches an employee, Esther, and says, "The supply closet is getting low on several items. I'm frustrated that you aren't keeping it stocked."

Esther responds, "I can't order any more supplies because we're already over our monthly budget."

"You should have come to me to request more budget, instead of just letting supply stock run out!" Steve exclaimed.

Their conversation escalates into a back-and-forth confrontational exchange, with no resolution achieved. Steve becomes aggravated because he wants and needs supplies. Esther is put on the defensive, even though she has no control over the budget.

When we interact with our coworkers or supervisors, we have the option to be reactive or to be intentional. Put another way, you and I have the option to be cranky or wise in how we respond to our bosses, coworkers, spouses, family members, and all others with whom we interact regularly.

This is determined by what part of your brain you decide to tap into, the lower (Crocodile) or upper (Wise Owl) sphere. You can make the decision to overcome your reactivity (crankiness) and be intentional and reasoned (wise) so you can then shift into being curious (growth).

When coworkers choose to be reactive in their conversations, it interferes with the productive flow of business, which comes at a cost in dollars and cents. Maybe hundreds or even millions of dollars and cents, depending on the size of the business. Remember the chapter on SC Dialogue in corporations. Think of it this way: being cranky can be costly. Let's try the reasoned and wise approach on for size instead. If you apply SC Dialogue to Steve and Esther's confrontational conversation, the reasoned and wise response for Esther to Steve would be first to mirror his statements, and then to ask him if she understands him correctly.

Esther: You noticed that the supply closet is getting low on some items and want to know why stock is low. Did I understand you correctly?

Steve: Yes, I have asked you to always keep at least

three of each item in stock, but there are several
items with less than three.

Esther: That makes sense. Now I understand why you're
upset. We are over budget for the month, so I am
waiting until the first of next month to restock. If you'd
like, I can ask our supervisor to request more funding
to stock the supply closet so we won't run out again.

Steve: Thanks, let's see if the supervisor agrees to that.
Thanks for helping work this out.

Instead of butting heads, Esther and Steve had a calm and civil
discussion that will likely lead to a productive resolution rather
than a reactive, cranky, and contentious argument that leads to
higher blood pressure levels and an unhealthy work environment.

CHOOSING HOW TO COMMUNICATE OVER A FRUSTRATION WITH A BOSS

Back in the gold rush days of the Old West, those panning
creeks and rivers for gold nuggets had to deal with claim jumpers
who horned in on their territory and tried to steal their mineral
rights to the gold found in the location of the claim.

The modern-day office version of that unethical practice
might be the "credit claimer." We all seem to have encountered
this sort of shameless coworker or supervisor who claims credit
for the good work of other people to enhance his or her own
climb up the corporate ladder, often at the expense of those who
really deserve to move up.

Here is an example.

Cranky Fred: Hey, Jason, the idea you presented in the
meeting about consolidating the sales and marketing

team meetings was my idea, and you presented it as your own! That was a jerk move!

Wise Fred: Hi, Jason. Are you available now to chat about the meeting earlier today? I wanted to talk about the idea you presented, the one about consolidating the sales and marketing team meetings. Is now a good time?

Wise Jason: I'm available now.

Wise Fred: I first want to express an appreciation. I really appreciate how you're able to clearly present new ideas in an exciting way.

Wise Jason: If I heard you correctly, you appreciate when I clearly present new ideas in an exciting way. Did I get that?

Wise Fred: Yes, you got that. And the upset I want to express is that today during our meeting, you didn't tell the group that I had suggested that idea to you.

Wise Jason: What I heard you say is that you're upset that I didn't tell the team that you came up with the idea of combining the sales and marketing team meetings. Did I get that? Do you have more to share?

Wise Fred: You got it right. No, that's the only issue I have for now.

Wise Jason: That makes sense. I understand why you're upset. I can imagine you may have felt betrayed when I didn't tell the team that you had come up with that idea. Is that how you feel?

Wise Fred: Yes, and thanks for understanding. Like

most people, I prefer to be recognized for my good ideas and good work, but you can feel free to take credit for any of my bad ideas and bad work in the future.

Okay, maybe that last remark was more wise guy than wise, but you get the idea. There are productive ways to deal with issues at work and in life if you are willing to let go of your right to be cranky and embrace your right to be wise.

Here is yet another example involving Andre and his boss, Mr. Alvarez:

Reactive Andre: Mr. Alvarez, every time I suggest an idea you ignore me. I quit!

Reasoned Andre: Hello, Mr. Alvarez, would now be a good time to discuss something with you?

Mr. Alvarez: Yes, now is a good time.

Reasoned Andre: First, I appreciate you giving me some time to talk about this situation. What I want to discuss is my experience that each time I present an idea, you refuse to acknowledge it. I get frustrated when I don't receive any feedback or acknowledgment.

Mr. Alvarez: Let me see if I understand you correctly. You appreciate my being available to talk with you about your experience when you present an idea. If I got that part, when you bring an idea to me, you experience me not acknowledging it and you are frustrated that you aren't receiving any feedback. Did I get that? Is there more?

Reasoned Andre: Yes, you got it. And no, I have no other issues to discuss.

Mr. Alvarez: That makes sense. I understand why you are frustrated. I understand you may feel like you aren't being seen or heard. Is that how you are feeling?

Reasoned Andre: Yes.

Mr. Alvarez: Thanks for telling me about this. You deserve to be acknowledged for your ideas, and I will do my best to acknowledge your ideas from now on.

Reasoned Andre: Thank you for hearing me and telling me you think my ideas deserve being acknowledged and that you will do so in the future.

CHOOSING HOW TO COMMUNICATE OVER A PERSONAL ISSUE AT WORK

Something as simple as expressing your feelings in a contained way that lands on authentic listening can shift the dynamics between an employer and employee. And here's an example of expressing frustrations in a nonreactive way between colleagues.

Reactive Danielle: Sophia, your constant pen clicking is driving me crazy! Stop being so annoying!

Reasoned Danielle: Hi, Sophia, are you free to talk right now about a frustration I have?

Sophia: Sure, I'm free to talk now.

Reasoned Danielle: Sophia, I appreciate how responsible you are with your projects and for making the time to talk with me about my frustration. What I want to share is that I'm sensitive to repetitive sounds, and I've noticed it's hard for me to concentrate on work when I hear your regular pen clicking.

Sophia: Let me see if I got it. You appreciate how responsible I am with my work. And you appreciate my willingness to take some time to talk about a frustration you have with me. If I got it, you want me to know that you are sensitive to repetitive sounds, and when I click my pen over and over, it's difficult for you to stay focused on work. Did I get that? Is there more?

Reasoned Danielle: Yes, you got it, and no, that is my only issue right now.

Sophia: That makes sense. I understand why you're struggling to concentrate. I can see how that continual sound could make you feel frustrated because your work is being interrupted. Is that how you feel?

Reasoned Danielle: Yes.

Sophia: I will do my best to stop clicking my pen. It's just a nervous habit when I'm concentrating, and I understand that you may find it distracting. I'll try to be aware of your sensitivity to repetitive sounds and not do it in your presence. Thanks for letting me know.

Reasoned Danielle: Thank you for understanding, Sophia.

SC Dialogue, as illustrated in the previous examples, not only allows you to talk to anyone about anything despite your differences, but it also creates a sense of safety that brings out the best in your upper Wise Owl Brain.

Healthy Brains, Healthy Relationships Summed Up

In recent years, neuroscientists have discovered there are strategic roles in the brain that go beyond basic survival. This neural system relies on our relationships with other members of our species for health and survival. Our physical survival is equated with the quality of our connecting with others.[6]

The sense of safety we feel in our healthy relationships enables our brains to foster positive social engagement along with nurturing and growth activities.

When safety reigns in our relationships, the lower brain can let down its guard, and our body begins to release endorphins and serotonin, which create a state of peace and relaxation. These neurochemicals released through the bloodstream are believed to contribute to healthier relationships, healthier bodies, and happier and longer lives.

When danger appears, our systems go on high alert and the primal brain sends out a distress signal. This prompts your adrenal glands to release a surge of hormones, including adrenaline and cortisol, which are toxic neurochemicals that make you anxious, angry, and even murderous.

Once you engage in the Safe Conversations skills, you can create a sense of safety. Your body relaxes, and your higher brain can fully function. Many of us think the magical phrase in our SC Dialogue process is this: "Is there more?" We believe this sentence stem is especially valuable because it helps people shift from judgment to curiosity and wonder. When we are in a state of wonder, we open our minds to new, deeper awareness of one another. Wonder washes our brains with neurochemicals that relax it and give it a longer life. There is always more, if we take the time, that ever expands this wonderful experience of deep relaxation and joyful connecting.

Conclusion

Once we listen more effectively so we understand one another's points of view, we can put aside our insistence that others agree with us. When we communicate by both talking and listening, we are more likely to grasp and understand the views and perspectives of others. When this happens, it nurtures a sense of caring and understanding between all parties involved in the dialogue. In these mutually respectful conversations, judgment can be eliminated in favor of curiosity about others and the world around us.

We believe the axis of history turns on *changing how we talk to each other.*

Given that belief, our goal over the next thirty years is to teach the SC Dialogue process to 2.5 billion persons, the tipping point of the world's projected population in 2050, with the intent of helping usher in the next and fourth stage in human social evolution.

This new stage will replace the third stage of human evolution, which we are in now, called the Age of the Individual. The third age replaced the second stage, called the Age of Agriculture.

Conclusion

The first stage was the Age of Tribalism. The Age of Relationship is our next step as a species to ensure we not only survive, but thrive. That will be a new global humanity.

Join the Vision of a New
Global Civilization

We believe that SC Dialogue is more than just a new way to communicate. It is the path to a new way of living together that will enhance all lives. We are all connected. The welfare of each of us is dependent upon the welfare of us all. That awareness gives birth to a new value system, and potentially to a new culture in which the health of couples, families, and individuals will be supported by transformed social systems that promote cooperation, collaboration, and equality, thus creating safety, connection, and joy as our shared humanity.

To achieve this, instead of our current polarized and contentious world, we ask you to imagine:

- a world filled with healthy and happy couples and thriving children who nurture and encourage each other!;
- safe schools without violence or fear, where children achieve academic excellence and keep their sense of wonder;
- corporations that place a priority on the relational well-being of all their employees and community members while creating jobs and flourishing financially;
- organizations that thrive and make the world a better place by harnessing the power of diverse opinions, perspectives, and talents;
- congregations where all members are connected,

supportive, empathic, and dedicated to making the world a better place for all;

- communities where everyone feels safe and connected and that are welcoming to all;
- political systems dedicated to the human values of freedom for all, universal equality, radical inclusiveness, and the celebration of diversity; and
- countries where war is a distant memory of a tragic age when people talked in monologues and competed with one another for control and dominance rather than cooperated for the welfare of all.

To achieve this vision requires that the SC Dialogue tools be applied to the following ecosystems:

- Families, so they become safe places where everyone feels protected and thrives, keeping the family intact and poverty at bay. This alone would prevent most personal and social problems.
- Classrooms, so they become places where all students connect when they are interacting and students make better grades.
- Congregations, so they help everyone connect around their similarities and differences.
- Workplaces, so they become locations where employees feel seen, heard, and valued (which affects the communities they serve) and their bottomline increases.
- Organizations, so they become resources for the communities they serve.
- First responders, so that they replace the use of force with positive social engagement.

Conclusion

- Criminal justice system, so that it shifts from a philosophy of punishment as justice to repairing the cognitive and emotional scars from childhood that produced the antisocial behavior that created the need for a criminal justice system.
- Prisons, so they become centers of relational well-being, where inmates are taught SC Dialogue to use for their benefit when they return to society.
- Social movements, so they replace polarization with positive social engagement.
- Political organizations, to help them respectfully embrace differences as opportunities to promote legislation for the benefit of all stakeholders.
- Professional organizations, in order to develop a philosophy of promoting relational well-being as the end goal of all their educational and implementation strategies.

We believe this is all possible because of a little-known fact: the way we talk to each other embodies a value system that evolves over time into the structures of social, political, economic, and religious institutions. SC Dialogue will create lateral human systems to replace the vertical one that uses monologue. Lateral human systems are safe and support freedom, equality, inclusion, and the celebration of difference for all.

In a relational world that values universal freedom, full equality for everyone, the celebration of difference, and total inclusiveness, a case could be made that all civilizations are people adapting to their environment, and all external changes change our brains.

Putting relationships first would restructure the neural circuits of the brain. We would eventually quiet the anxious, reactive

Crocodile Brain and grow the empathic Wise Owl Brain so we can live a life marked by wonder and peace, thus creating more evolved human beings who can live together in community.

Putting relationships first also challenges the default position of the brain, which puts self-interest first. Our brains are social, and connecting is our foundational reality. The welfare of the whole serves the interest of individuals. This radicalizes all interactions in all human ecosystems, making relationship first an ethical practice.

Spread the Word

We encourage you to use the sentence stems of SC Dialogue in your daily life, whether in your personal relationships, a planning meeting with your boss and coworkers, when discussing growth strategies with your fellow congregation members at your church or designing legislative initiatives with your fellow constituents.

Armed with the tools of Safe Conversations, *you* can be part of a global transformation by applying them to every facet of your life. We invite you to create a ripple effect that will help all of us grow toward a world of complete peace and joy where SC Dialogue is the new human language, replacing monologue. Then we can all talk to one another and be supportive and productive despite our differences.

As SC Dialogue becomes practiced more widely, the methodology can help transform the value systems by which we live. We hope to see our collective consciousness evolve from the individual self and independence toward one of greater interdependency with a stronger sense of community.

While promoting the welfare of the individual has furthered

Conclusion

human evolution over the last three hundred years, shifting to relationship first supports the next phase of human evolution by making all relationships important. Finally, putting relationships first serves as a catalyst of a new community based on a relational value system as a way of life, a way of being with others.

A world community with that priority would transcend any that was organized around the individual. This is how we can live together and thrive in all our interactions with others.

What a world that will be!

Additional Resources

For relational educational opportunities by Harville and Helen, please visit www.HarvilleandHelen.com where you can:

- purchase books, e-books, and online courses;
- discover writings, podcasts, and invitations to special events, including live teleseminars with Harville and Helen;
- find updates on Harville and Helen's workshop and lecture schedule; and
- participate in a global mission of creating healthy relationships.

Quantum Connections brings the transformative power of Safe Conversations® Dialogue Methodology and Tools to small businesses, large corporations, global faith communities, educational institutions, and community organizations, along with individuals, couples, and families. Based in the neuro and quantum social sciences, Quantum Connections delivers comprehensive and highly structured training programs designed to foster the use of essential SC Dialogue skills in all interpersonal interactions—empowering people to talk to one another without criticism and listen without judgment to connect beyond difference. Our customers gain measurable value as high-performing teams eliminate silos and traditional company and cultural boundaries and move the organization from monologue to dialogue, which will, ultimately, result in significantly improved levels of employee engagement, retention, and inclusivity.

Developed and refined over four decades, the Safe Conversations Dialogue Methodology and Tools that form the foundation of Quantum Connections' training programs are the intellectual property of founders Harville Hendrix, PhD, and Helen LaKelly Hunt, PhD. Together, the proven methodology, time-tested tools, and skill-development practices used in Quantum Connections programs serve as the basis for the founders' bestselling book, *Getting the Love You Want*, with more than four million copies sold worldwide since 1988.

www.QuantumConnections.com

Imago Relationships International (IRI) was cofounded by Harville Hendrix, PhD, and Helen LaKelly Hunt, PhD, to help couples and individuals create strong and fulfilling relationships. More than twenty-five hundred certified Imago Therapists are available in more than sixty countries. IRI is dedicated to providing the very best resources for therapists and laypersons seeking training to develop proficiency in the Imago relational method. The Imago Clinical and Facilitator Training will provide you with an overview of the theory and essential skills for working with relationships.

www.ImagoRelationships.org

Acknowledgments

The completion of any book is always a function of people other than its authors. In this case, we are deeply indebted to many people whose contributions were essential for this book to come to fruition.

Of course, as an Imago advocate, Oprah Winfrey gets the top mention, as she gave Imago and the Dialogue Process global visibility in 1988 by featuring our book, *Getting the Love You Want: A Guide for Couples*, on *The Oprah Winfrey Show* and then showcasing it seventeen more times over the next twenty years.

Given global visibility by Oprah, many therapists joined the Imago clinical training program. Among the earliest were Eugene Shelly, Wendy Palmer Patterson, and Maya Kollman, each of whom adopted dialogue as a therapeutic process. Later, Al Turtle and Orli Wahrman, Imago therapists, were among those who moved the SC Dialogue process out of the clinic into the public, as well as the group dialogue process called Communologue, which they implemented in a variety of nonclinical settings, including peace talks between nations, negotiations in unions and

Acknowledgments

communities, and in corporations and universities. Appreciation also goes to Bob Patterson, who was the first to language Imago as a social mission in his now-famous and globally adopted phrase: "transforming the world, one couple at a time."

While this book was given form by us, the inspiration and content within it is a product of a community of professional colleagues, businesses, educational and therapy professionals, and couples with whom we have been in conversation, for decades, about the transformative power of SC Dialogue. Again, to list everyone who inspired us, those who supported us, and all who contributed their experience and wisdom would create a list too long for this page, and we would no doubt leave someone out. So we decided to name only the select few who were hands-on in helping with the actual research, writing, management, and production of the book.

First among those is Wes Smith, our writing partner, whose organizational skills, research savvy, and creative pen gave the book its literary style. With deep intelligence, Wes comprehended the concept and scope of the book. And with an artistic command of language, he has made an abstract concept and complex methodology accessible to both the professional world and the general public, moving SC Dialogue toward becoming a new way of talking for everyone and ushering in a new relational civilization.

Second is Sanam Hoon, who, for over thirty years, has managed the complexity of our professional lives and supported all our projects, like this one. In this case, Sanam not only helped keep the book on schedule and interfaced with the publishers on many details, but she also secured most of the stories that populate the book. Without her, the richness of the personal story would have been missing.

Next, we would like to acknowledge the many people from the

Safe Conversations and Imago communities who shared their stories with us. They made the book a living testament of the power of the Safe Conversations process. While not all their musings made it to this book, they all informed the work and nuances along the way. These include (but are not limited to): Clay and Sonja Arnold, Helit Assa, Pollyanna and Baldwin Barnes, Michael and Nancy Bryant, Mo Byers, John Castranova, Ronald A. Clark, Michael DiPaolo, Cassie Guerin, Morella Hammer, Robin Hills, Michael Kaufmann, James Kennedy, Maya Kollman, David Lawson, Deborah Lindholm and Samuel Mayson, Carlee Myers, Jolena Nicol and Burger Pretorius, Rev. Doc Lisa, Rabbi Elana Rosen-Brown, David Rudnick, Sonali Sadequee, Jose Soto, Meira Tamir, Al Turtle, Jen Urano, Orli Wahrman, and LaSheryl Walker.

A special acknowledgment goes to Charlotte Legg, who not only was integral in the growth of the Safe Conversations community of leaders, but also helped capture their stories. Her passionate belief in our work has been unwavering.

Another special acknowledgment goes to Laura Davis, an executive at JPMorgan in NYC, who supported this project from its beginning many years ago.

We are also deeply grateful to Dan Siegel and Caroline Welch for not only contributing to the foreword of this book, but also for their friendship and expert guidance on interpersonal neurobiology.

And without a publishing team, there is no book! Austin Miller from Dupree Miller and Associates (DMA) became our literary agent. He and DMA's founder and CEO, Jan Miller, grasped our vision from the outset and found the perfect home with W Publishing Group. At W, we would like to thank Associate Publisher Stephanie C. Newton and Senior Editor Lauren Bridges, who took great care in providing feedback to our manuscript, as well as making it a dialogical experience.

Acknowledgments

And lastly, but certainly not least, we would like to thank Dennis S. Holland, the CEO of our organization, now called Quantum Connections. Under his leadership, we were able to get the Safe Conversations methodology and tools into all ecosystems and set it on an upward trajectory, inching closer to our vision of a truly relational civilization.

Notes

INTRODUCTION

1. Oprah's Super Soul Sunday, "Alanis Morissette on Oprah's Super Soul Sunday Discussing Safe Conversations," *Vimeo WFAA Production*, October 18, 2018, https://vimeo.com/295856819.
2. Liz Mineo, "Good genes are nice, but joy is better," *The Harvard Gazette,* April 11, 2017, https://news.harvard.edu/gazette/story/2017/04/over-nearly-80-years-harvard-study-has-been-showing-how-to-live-a-healthy-and-happy-life/.

CHAPTER 1

1. David Smith, "It's just gotten crazy: how the origins of Covid became a toxic US political debate," *The Guardian*, February 28, 2023, https://www.theguardian.com/world/2023/feb/28/lab-leak-natural-spillover-how-origins-covid-us-political-debate.
2. William G. Gale and Darrell M. West, "Another Civil War?" Brookings Institution, September 16, 2021, https://www.brookings.edu/articles/is-the-us-headed-for-another-civil-war/.
3. Gale and West, "Is the US headed for another Civil War?"
4. Marnie Hunter, "FAA numbers confirm it—2021 was terrible for bad behavior in the skies," CNN, updated January 13, 2022, https://www.cnn.com/travel/article/unruly-airline-passengers-faa-2021/index.html.

5. Hunter, "FAA Numbers Confirm It."

6. Jenn Brown, "The Art of Listening: An Interview with Harville Hendrix and Helen LaKelly Hunt," Be Here Now Network, 2019, https://beherenownetwork.com/the-art-of-listening-an-interview-with-harville-hendrix-and-helen-lakelly-hunt/.

7. Carlo Rovelli, *Helgoland: Making Sense of the Quantum Revolution* (New York: Riverhead Books, 2021).

8. William Wordsworth, "Ode: Intimations of Immortality from Recollections of Early Childhood," in *Poems in Two Volumes*, ed. Helen Darbishire (Oxford: Clarendon Press, 1952), 321–332.

9. Edward Tronick, "Still Face Experiment," YouTube, uploaded July 27, 2022, http://www.youtube.com/watch?v=f1Jw0-LExyc.

10. Kirk J. Schneider and Sayyed Mohsen Fatemi, "Today's Biggest Threat: The Polarized Mind," *Scientific American*, April 16, 2019, https://blogs.scientificamerican.com/observations/todays-biggest-threat-the-polarized-mind/.

11. Gavin Evans, "'Be Like Mike': The Story Behind Michael Jordan's Iconic Gatorade Commercial Song," Complex.com, May 6, 2018, https://www.complex.com/sports/a/gavin-evans/be-like-mike-michael-jordan-gatorade-commercial-song.

12. A. H. Maslow, "A Theory of Human Motivation," *Psychological Review* 50, no. 4 (1943): 370–96, APA PsychNet, https://psycnet.apa.org/doi/10.1037/h0054346.

13. T. Hutman and M. Dapretto, "The Emergence of Empathy During Infancy," *Cognition, Brain, Behavior: An Interdisciplinary Journal* 13, no. 4 (2009): 367–90, APA PsychNet, https://psycnet.apa.org/record/2009–24085–002.

CHAPTER 2

1. Martin Buber, *I and Thou*, trans. Walter Kaufmann (New York: Touchstone, 1996).

CHAPTER 3

1. Lydia Denworth, "Making Eye Contact Signals a New Turn in a Conversation," *Scientific American,* September 21, 2021, https://www.scientificamerican.com/article/making-eye-contact-signals-a-new-turn-in-a-conversation.

CHAPTER 4

1. Tara Van Bommel, "The Power of Empathy in Times of Crisis and Beyond," Catalyst, 2021, https://www.catalyst.org/reports /empathy-work-strategy-crisis/.
2. Van Bommel, "The Power of Empathy."
3. Nelle Morton, "The Rising Woman Consciousness in Male Language Structure," *Andover Newton Quarterly* (Andover Newton Theological School, University of Illinois at Urbana-Champaign, March 1972): 171–90.

CHAPTER 5

1. Kathryn P. Brooks and Christine Dunkel Schetter, "Social Negativity and Health: Conceptual and Measurement Issues," *Social and Personality Psychology* 5, no. 11 (November 2011): Compass, https://doi.org/10.1111/j.1751–9004.2011.00395.x.
2. Rick Hanson, *Buddha's Brain: The Practical Neuroscience of Happiness, Love & Wisdom* (Oakland, CA: New Harbinger Publications, 2009) 40–45.

CHAPTER 6

1. Harvard Medical School, "Giving thanks can make you happier," Harvard Health Publishing, August 14, 2021, https://www.health .harvard.edu/healthbeat/giving-thanks-can-make-you-happier.
2. Harvard Medical School, "Giving thanks."

CHAPTER 7

1. Elizabeth Perry, "What is neuroplasticity and why is it important?" BetterUp (blog), September 29, 2021, https://www.betterup.com /blog/what-is-neuroplasticity.
2. Louis J. Cozolino, *The Neuroscience of Human Relationships: Attachment and the Developing Social Brain*, 2nd ed. (New York: W. W. Norton & Company, 2014).
3. Daniel J. Siegel, *The Mindful Brain: Reflection and Attunement in the Cultivation of Well-Being* (New York: W. W. Norton & Company, 2007).
4. M. Grawitch, M. Gottschalk, and D. C. Munz, "The Path to a Healthy Workplace: A Critical Review Linking Healthy

Workplace Practices, Employee Well-being, and Organizational Improvements," *Consulting Psychology Journal Practice and Research*, 58, no. 3 (2006): 129–47, APA PsycNet, https://psycnet .apa.org/doiLanding?doi=10.1037%2F1065–9293.58.3.129.

CHAPTER 8

1. Robert Fulghum, *All I Really Need to Know I Learned in Kindergarten: Uncommon Thoughts on Common Things* (New York: Ivy, 1988).

CHAPTER 9

1. Amanda May Agathagelou, "Individual Psychodynamic Development: The Imago Relationship Approach in Organisational Context" (PhD diss., University of South Africa, September 2013), https://uir.unisa.ac.za/bitstream /handle/10500/13371/thesis_agathagelou_am.pdf.

2. Rebecca Sears, "Managing Group Diversity: Communologue Training," The Imago Center, accessed April 17, 2024, https:// imagocenterdc.com/managing-group-diversity-communologue -training.

3. Max Zahn, "Puerto Rico's power grid is struggling 5 years after Hurricane Maria. Here's why," ABC News, September 22, 2022, https://abcnews.go.com/Technology/puerto-ricos-power-grid -struggling-years-hurricane-maria/story?id=90151141.

4. Nishant Kishore et al., "Mortality in Puerto Rio after Hurricane Maria," *New England Journal of Medicine* 379, no. 2, (July 2018): 162–70, https://doi.org/10.1056/NEJMsa1803972.

5. Margaret J. Wheatley, *Turning to One Another: Simple Conversations to Restore Hope to the Future* (San Francisco: Berrett-Koehler, 2014).

6. "Liberia: Foundation for Woman Partners with Change Agent Network to Introduce Safe Conversations to Liberia," *FrontPage Africa*, news release, November 21, 2022, https:// frontpageafricaonline.com/news/liberia-foundation-for-women -partners-with-change-agent-network-to-introduce-safe -conversations-to-liberia/.

7. Simeon Wiakanty, "Liberia: Foundation for Women Embark[s] on Dialogue Series Safe Conversations," *Daily Observer*, July 18,

2023, https://www.liberianobserver.com/liberia-foundation
-women-embark-dialogue-series-safe-conversations.

8. Will at DJ Raw Productions, "Safe Conservations in Liberia,"
YouTube video, 4:49, December 21, 2021, https://www.youtube
.com/watch?v=TB4vdjrVFJs.

9. Donald Gibbon, "An Application of Communologue: United Way
of Kootenai County," Al Turtle, November 11, 2006, https://
www.alturtle.com/archives/970.

10. Donald Gibbon, "The Israeli-Palestinian Imago Project," Imago
RLI, 2007, https://www.imagorli.co.il/an-introduction-to-imago
/the-israeli-palestinian-imago-project.

11. Gibbon, "The Israeli-Palestinian Imago Project."

12. Gibbon.

13. Gibbon.

14. Orli Wahrman, interview by Sanam Hoon, March 28, 2023.

15. Wahrman, interview; Orli Wahrman, email to Sanam Hoon,
November 28, 2023.

16. Gibbon, "The Israeli-Palestinian Imago Project."

CHAPTER 10

1. Peter Amato, "The Blow-By-Blow on Remote Work Conflict,"
My Perfect Resume.com [2021 Study], accessed April 17, 2024,
https://www.myperfectresume.com/career-center/careers/basics
/remote-work-conflict.

2. Helen LaKelly Hunt, "Safe Conversations and Corporations: A
Stronger Bottom Line and More Gender Equity," April 8, 2020,
https://static.safeconversations.com/sc1/2020/05/09141439/safe
-conversations-and-corporations_a-stronger-bottom-line-and
-more-gender-equity.pdf.

3. Jim Harter, "U.S. Employee Engagement Needs a Rebound in
2023," Gallup, January 25, 2023, https://www.gallup.com
/workplace/468233/employee-engagement-needs-rebound-2023.
aspx; *State of the Global Workplace: 2023 Report*, Gallup, 2023,
https://www.gallup.com/workplace/349484/state-of-the-global
-workplace.aspx.

4. Harter, "U.S. Employee Engagement."

5. Harter.

6. Elaine Houston, "The Importance of Positive Relationships in

the Workplace," Positive Psychology, December 30, 2019, https://
positivepsychology.com/positive-relationships-workplace/.

7. David Grossman, "The Cost of Poor Communications," *Holmes Report* (blog), PRovoke Media, July 16, 2011, https://www
.provokemedia.com/latest/article/the-cost-of-poor
-communications, in "The Cost of Poor Communications: The
Business Rationale for Building This Critical Competency," Society
for Human Resource Management, February 19, 2016, https://
www.shrm.org/topics-tools/news/cost-poor-communications.

8. Prudy Gourguechon, "Start the New Year by Learning to Avoid
Bad Business Relationships," *Forbes*, January 1, 2018, https://
www.forbes.com/sites/prudygourguechon/2018/01/01/start-the
-new-year-by-learning-to-avoid-bad-business-relationships.

9. Josh Bivens and Jori Kandra, "CEO pay has skyrocketed 1,460%
since 1978," Economic Policy Institute, October 4, 2022, https://
www.epi.org/publication/ceo-pay-in-2021/.

10. Charles Duhigg, "What Google Learned from Its Quest to Build
the Perfect Team," *New York Times*, February 25, 2016, https://
www.nytimes.com/2016/02/28/magazine/what-google-learned
-from-its-quest-to-build-the-perfect-team.html.

11. Hanson, *Buddha's Brain*, 40–42.

12. Hanson, 40–42.

13. M. Grawitch, M. Gottschalk, and D. C. Munz, "Healthy
workplace."

14. Benjamin Laker, "Culture Is a Company's Single Most Powerful
Advantage. Here's Why," *Forbes*, April 23, 2021, https://www
.forbes.com/sites/benjaminlaker/2021/04/23/culture-is-a
-companys-single-most-powerful-advantage-heres-why/?sh=
4aee2b88679e.

15. Daniel J. Siegel, *The Mindful Brain*.

16. Hunt, "Safe Conversations and Corporations."

CHAPTER 11

1. Kelly Bilodeau, "Fostering Healthy Relationships," Harvard
Health, July 1, 2021, https://www.health.harvard.edu/mind-and
-mood/fostering-healthy-relationships.

2. "11 Fun Facts about Your Brain," Northwestern Medicine,

October 2019, https://www.nm.org/healthbeat/healthy-tips/11
-fun-facts-about-your-brain.

3. F. Vazza and A. Feletti, "The Quantitative Comparison Between the Neuronal Network and the Cosmic Web," *Frontiers in Physics* 16, November 2020, https://doi.org/10.3389/fphy.2020 .525731.

4. Seymour Boorstein, *Who's Talking Now: The Owl or The Crocodile* (Bloomington, IN: AuthorHouse, 2011).

5. Mayfield Brain & Spine, "Anatomy of the Brain," Mayfield Clinic, updated April 2018, https://mayfieldclinic.com/pe -anatbrain.htm.

CHAPTER 12

1. Liz Mineo, "Good Genes Are Nice, but Joy Is Better," *Harvard Gazette*, April 11, 2017, https://news.harvard.edu/gazette/story /2017/04/over-nearly-80-years-harvard-study-has-been-showing -how-to-live-a-healthy-and-happy-life/.

2. Maggie Woods, "Civic Conversations—Building Relationships One Conversation at a Time," Community Engagement Learning Exchange (blog), University of North Carolina, August 4, 2019, https://cele.sog.unc.edu/civic-conversations-building-relationships -one-conversation-at-a-time/.

3. Woods, "Civic Conversations"; Braver Angels, accessed January 3, 2024, https://braverangels.org/.

4. Aristotle, "Book VIII" in *Nicomachean Ethics*, trans. Roger Crisp (Cambridge University Press, 2014), 141.

5. Anika Prather, "Understanding Friendship Through the Eyes of Aristotle," Antigone Journal, March 2021, https://antigonejourna l.com/2021/03/understanding-friendship-through-aristotle/.

6. Tao de Haas, "The Brain in Relationships," About My Brain (blog), October 31, 2010, https://www.aboutmybrain.com/blog /the-brain-in-relationships.

About the Authors

Harville Hendrix, PhD, began his career as a therapist and educator at the Pastoral Counseling Center of Greater Chicago in 1965, where he was clinical director. He received his doctorate in psychology and theology in 1970 and became a member of the faculty of Perkins Divinity School at Southern Methodist University in Dallas, Texas, where he taught for nine years. In 1979, he entered private practice as a therapist.

In 1977, Harville met Helen LaKelly Hunt, and they married in 1982. They are cocreators of Imago Relationship Therapy, a couple's therapy, and coauthors of three *New York Times* bestsellers (*Getting the Love You Want, Keeping the Love You Find*, and *Giving the Love That Heals*), *Receiving Love, Making Marriage Simple, Doing Imago Relationship Therapy in the Space-Between*, and six other books on relationships. Imago Relationship Therapy has been featured on *The Oprah Winfrey Show* seventeen times, one of which won for her the "Most Socially Redemptive" Award for daytime talk shows. It has also been featured on many other major television and radio shows and in countless newspapers and major magazines.

Harville and Helen founded the Institute for Imago Relationship Therapy to train therapists in the Imago process and to develop workshops for couples and singles. Later called the Imago International Training Institute, which has forty faculty members, the Institute has trained over twenty-five hundred therapists who practice Imago Relationship Therapy in over sixty countries, and nearly two hundred workshop presenters who conduct workshops around the world. These Imago professionals founded Imago Relationships Worldwide for professional growth and development and created an international Imago community.

In 2015, Harville and Helen cofounded an organization called Safe Conversations LLC, now Quantum Connections. This training institute teaches a relational intervention called Safe Conversations Dialogue, which is based on the latest relational sciences that can help anyone shift from conflict to connection. Harville and Helen believe that Safe Conversations methodology and tools can contribute to a more relational world, with more gender and racial equity. To that end, the aim of Quantum Connections is to teach Safe Conversations methodology and tools to 2.5 billion people (the tipping point of the world population in 2050) over the next thirty years, with the intention of facilitating that shift from our current "individualistic" civilization to a relational civilization, the fourth stage in human social evolution.

Harville is a graduate of Mercer University in Macon, Georgia, which awarded him an Honorary Doctorate of Human Letters. He holds a master of divinity from Union Theological Seminary in New York and an MA and a PhD in psychology and religion from the School of Divinity at the University of Chicago. Dr. Hendrix is the recipient of several honors, including the Outstanding Pastoral Counselor of the Year Award (1995) from the American Baptist Churches, the 1995 Distinguished Contribution Award from the American Association of Pastoral Counselors, and, jointly with Helen, the Distinguished Contributors Award from the Association for Imago Relationship Therapy. A Diplomate in the American Association of Pastoral Counselors, he has been a clinical member of the American Group Psychotherapy Association and the International Transactional Analysis Association, and is a former board member of the Group Psychotherapy Foundation.

Harville and Helen have a blended family of six children and eight grandchildren. They live and work in Dallas, Texas, and New York City.

Helen LaKelly Hunt, PhD, earned her doctorate in women's history from Union Theological Seminary in New York. She is a cocreator with her husband, Harville Hendrix, of Imago Relationship Theory & Therapy and cofounder of the Imago International Training Institute, which has a teaching faculty of forty members; and of Imago Relationships Worldwide, which supports the growth and practice of Imago Relationship Therapy in over sixty countries by over twenty-five hundred therapists.

In 2015, Helen cofounded with Harville an organization called Safe Conversations LLC, now known as Quantum Connections. This training institute teaches Safe Conversations methodology and tools, a relational intervention based on the latest relational sciences that can help anyone shift from conflict to connection. Helen believes that Safe Conversations can contribute to a more relational world, with more gender and racial equity.

In addition to her partnerships with Harville in the cocreation and distribution of Imago Relationship Therapy and

About the Authors

Safe Conversations, Helen is one of a small army of women who helped seed and develop the global women's movement. She cofounded the Texas Women's Foundation, the New York Women's Foundation, the Women's Funding Network, and Women Moving Millions. For her achievements, she was inducted into the National Women's Hall of Fame in 1994 for her contribution to the global women's movement and into the Smithsonian Institute for creating Women Moving Millions and her leadership in creative women's philanthropy.

Helen is sole author of *Faith and Feminism: A Holy Alliance*. Her latest book, *And the Spirit Moved Them: The Lost Radical History of America's First Feminists*, shares the inspiring story of the abolitionist feminists. Given her great interest in psychology, she has coauthored several books with her husband, Harville Hendrix, on Imago Therapy. These include three *New York Times* bestsellers (*Getting the Love You Want, Keeping the Love You Find*, and *Giving the Love That Heals*), *Receiving Love, Making Marriage Simple, Doing Imago Relationship Therapy in the Space-Between*, and six other books.